SON OF SAM CASE

SIMON & SCHUSTER INC. V. MEMBERS OF NY STATE CRIME VICTIMS BOARD

FIRST AMENDMENT CASES

SON OF SAM CASE

SIMON & SCHUSTER INC. V. MEMBERS OF NEW YORK STATE CRIME VICTIMS BOARD

By Susan Dudley Gold

Cavendish
Square

New York

With special thanks to Catherine McGlone, Esq. for reviewing the text of this book.

This publication represents the opinions and views of the author based on his or her personal experience, knowledge, and research. The information in this book serves as a general guide only. The author and publisher have used their best efforts in preparing this book and disclaim liability rising directly or indirectly from the use and application of this book.

CPSIA Compliance Information:
Batch #WW14CSQ

All websites were available and accurate when this book was sent to press.

LIBRARY OF CONGRESS CATALOGING-IN-PUBLICATION DATA

Gold, Susan Dudley, author. Son of Sam case : Simon and Schuster v. Members of United States Crime Victims Board / Susan Dudley Gold. pages cm. — (First amendment cases) Includes bibliographical references and index.
ISBN 978-1-62712-399-0 (hardcover)
ISBN 978-1-62712-400-3 (paperback)
ISBN 978-1-62712-401-0 (ebook)
1. Simon and Schuster, inc.—Trials, litigation, etc.—Juvenile literature. 2. New York (State). Crime Victims Board.—Trials, litigation, etc.—Juvenile literature. 3. Pileggi, Nicholas. Wiseguy—Juvenile literature. 4. Freedom of expression—United States—Juvenile literature. 5. Reparation (Criminal justice)—New York (State)—Juvenile literature. 6. Criminals' writings—Economic aspects—United States—Juvenile literature. I. Title. KF228.S543G65 2014 344.7303'56—dc23 2013033266

Art Director: Anahid Hamparian
Series Designer: Michael Nelson
Photo research: Custom Communications, Inc.

The photographs in this book are used by permission and through the courtesy of: Alamy: Vince Clements, cover; Dan Callister, 12, 96; AF archive, 20; National Geographic Image Collection, 51. Associated Press, 2 (bottom), 24, 57, 80, 100; Charles Tasnadi, 60; Rich Pedroncelli, 93; Mike Groll, 103; Nati Harnik, 111. Corbis: Bettman, 8, 86; Jacques M. Chenet, 68. Getty: Nick Sorrentino/NY Daily News, 15; Jon Levy/AFP, 28; Yvonne Hemsey, 30; Rebecca Sapp/WireImage, 47; Lee Balterman/Time & Life Pictures/Getty Images, 55. Everett Collection: 32. Library of Congress: Harris & Ewing Collection, 39. Newscom: AFP/Getty Images, 112.

Printed in the United States of America

CONTENTS

FIRST AMENDMENT

THE FIRST AMENDMENT

Congress shall make no law respecting an establishment of religion, or prohibiting the free exercise thereof; or abridging the freedom of speech, or of the press; or the right of the people peaceably to assemble, and to petition the Government for a redress of grievances.

—*U.S. Constitution, Amendment I*

Free Speech for All

IN A YEARLONG REIGN OF TERROR THAT BEGAN in the summer of 1976, a killer armed with a .44-caliber revolver and the moniker "Son of Sam" stalked victims in the New York City boroughs of Queens and the Bronx. He shot couples in parked cars and women walking home at night, creating a panic among New Yorkers. During the rampage, fearful residents avoided secluded streets at night, and women wore wigs or hats in the mistaken belief that the killer attacked only those with long, dark hair. Officials launched the largest manhunt in the city's history, involving hundreds of officers and the creation of a special task force devoted to apprehending the killer. By the time police arrested Son of Sam, a twenty-four-year-old postal worker named David R. Berkowitz, on August 10, 1977, he had shot six people to death and wounded seven others.

Berkowitz confessed to the attacks and received a sentence of 364 years in jail with no possibility of parole. Berkowitz never went to trial. Many questioned his sanity after he told officials that he had embarked on the

Officials lead David Berkowitz (*center*) to court in 1977 after the twenty-four-year-old postal worker was arrested as a suspect in the Son of Sam murders.

killing spree under orders from his neighbor Sam's black Labrador retriever.

The explosive nature of Berkowitz's crimes and the extensive publicity devoted to them fueled speculation that the killer would be well paid for firsthand accounts of his activities. Reportedly, a member of the media had boasted that a taped interview with Berkowitz would sell for $250,000. Within two days of Berkowitz's arrest, the New York state legislature enacted a law barring criminals from profiting from any book or movie about their crimes. In presenting his bill to the legislature, New York state senator Emanuel R. Gold told fellow lawmakers, "It is abhorrent to one's sense of justice and decency that an individual . . . can expect to receive large sums of money for his story once he is captured—while . . . people are dead, [and] other people were injured as a result of his conduct." Gold presented the bill to the legislature during the manhunt for Son of Sam after reading a newspaper article speculating that, once captured, the unknown killer "stood to get rich" from media deals.

Under the New York law, a criminal forfeited any money earned from a book or movie or other product depicting his or her crimes. Instead, the money went into a secure fund, called an escrow account, overseen by New York's Crime Victims Compensation Board (later the Crime Victims Board). An escrow account is a special fund in which money or other valuables are set aside for a particular reason (in this case, to offer some compensation to crime victims). Victims had five years after the signing of a contract for a book or a film about a given crime to claim the money in the escrow account. If no one filed a claim within that time, the money went to the criminal. During consideration of the bill, the state's Criminal Justice Services Division issued a memo noting that well-publicized crimes often brought criminals "a considerable amount of money" from books, television shows, and other productions. The bill sought "to redirect the money flow from the criminal to his victims."

The original law applied only to criminals convicted

in court. Since Berkowitz was found incompetent to stand trial, the escrow and forfeiture provisions did not apply to him. Nevertheless, the legislation of 1977 and similar regulations in other states became known as "Son of Sam" laws. Berkowitz voluntarily turned over his share of royalties from *Son of Sam*, Lawrence D. Klausner's book about his crimes, based in part on Berkowitz's diaries and published in 1981, even though he was not legally bound to do so. The money (approximately $120,000) went to the estates of the people killed by Berkowitz and to those who had survived his attacks. The New York law was later broadened to apply to anyone who admitted to crimes in books or movies as well as to people accused of crimes but never convicted.

Son of Sam laws bolstered the well-accepted tenet that crime should not pay. Few had sympathy for criminals who sought to get rich by recounting the details of horrendous crimes they had committed. While most people did not question the right of criminals to free speech, they supported the principle promoted by the Son of Sam laws that criminals should not be able to profit from accounts of their crimes, especially when victims went uncompensated. However, some people believed that the laws, by withholding royalties and other payments, interfered with criminals' freedom of speech.

New York became the center of the controversy swirling over the Son of Sam laws because many of the nation's publishers operated there. Crime and criminals have always piqued the public interest. Publishers know this and offer big advance payments for the privilege of printing criminals' stories. Press coverage of the crime, the investigation, and the trial often increases the public's interest in the story.

When Simon & Schuster, one of the world's largest publishers, released *Wiseguy*, a detailed account of the lives of some organized crime figures, the state confiscated the money paid to the criminal on whose reports the book was based. The confiscation occurred in 1985, and the matter eventually came before the U.S. Supreme Court. The 1991 ruling in *Simon & Schuster v. New York State Crime Victims Board* struck down New York's Son of Sam law and reaffirmed the doctrine of free speech for all. It also challenged states to devise other laws to address the legitimate goal of preventing criminals from benefiting from their crimes.

Henry Hill's royalties for his work on a biographical book about his exploits as a mob underling triggered the case that led to a landmark decision in *Simon & Schuster v. New York State Crime Victims Board* in 1991.

CHAPTER ONE

WISEGUYS AND GOODFELLAS

IN 1980 HENRY HILL JR., AN UNDERLING IN AN organized crime syndicate in New York, agreed to testify against the members of the Lucchese family, who controlled the Brooklyn, New York, neighborhood where he had grown up. The son of a Sicilian mother and an Irish father, the young Hill had longed to be a part of the gangster world he viewed across the street. Because of his mixed heritage, he could never become a full-fledged member of the Italian-run Mafia, but by age eleven he had gained the favor of mob chief Paul Vario, who gave him small tasks to perform. At sixteen Hill was arrested for credit card theft, but he won Vario's respect when he refused to give the police any information about his associates. The following year Hill joined the army and served for three years at a base in North Carolina. After he was discharged in 1963, he resumed his relationship with his gangster friends, embarking on a life of crime that included robbery, extortion, truck hijacking, loan-sharking, and burying bodies. Hill denied actually killing anyone but admitted to "breaking heads" of people targeted by the mob and burying bodies others had killed. Police once estimated that more than $100 million passed through his hands. He said he spent most of the money on "slow horses [betting on losing horses], drugs, and rock and roll."

In 1974 Hill began serving a ten-year sentence for extortion in a federal penitentiary, where he sold drugs to fellow inmates. When he got out on parole, he continued his drug trafficking activities despite Vario's ban on drug deals. The mob boss had ordered his underlings to stay away from the drug trade because those arrested for such crimes faced long prison sentences, and the temptation to testify against the Mafia in return for reduced prison time would be strong. Hill's defiance soured his relationship with Vario.

Through contacts, Hill learned that a shipment of jewels and cash would be stored in the Lufthansa cargo hold at John F. Kennedy International Airport in New York. He passed along the tip to his mob pal Jimmy "the Gent" Burke. On December 10, 1978, five hooded gangsters walked into the Lufthansa cargo area and grabbed $5.8 million in jewelry and unmarked bills. At the time,

An employee gestures to the spot where he and his coworkers were tied up during a robbery at the Lufthansa cargo area at John F. Kennedy International Airport.

it was the largest robbery of cash in American history. Soon, however, Burke's partners in the crime began dying, one by one. Hill said that Burke, the mastermind of the heist, had ordered death for the entire gang and anyone else who could link him to the crime.

Although he had not participated in the heist himself, Hill realized he could well be on Burke's list of those to be terminated. A drug dealer who had become an addict, Hill was arrested in May 1980 and charged with drug trafficking. His wife also faced charges as an accessory. Ironically, the arrest provided an escape route.

NEW YORK'S SON OF SAM LAW, 1986

By 1986 New York had amended its Son of Sam law three times after its initial enactment in 1977. The revised law allowed money in the escrow account to be used to pay the criminal's attorney fees first (but not more than one-fifth of the total funds in the account), then to reimburse the state for money paid to the criminal's victims. Escrow money also went to pay court-ordered damages to victims and to settle debts owed other creditors. The law defined a criminal as any person convicted of a crime in the state, anyone pleading guilty to a New York crime, and anyone who "voluntarily and intelligently" admitted to a crime in the state. This last provision covered people who said in a book or other work that they had committed crimes for which they were never prosecuted.

The revised law required:

> [Each] legal entity contracting with any person or the representative or assignee of any person, accused or convicted of a crime in this state, with respect to the reenactment of such crime, by way of a movie, book, magazine article, tape recording, phonograph record, radio or television presentation, live entertainment of any kind, or from the expression of such accused or convicted person's thoughts, feelings, opinions or emotions regarding such crime, shall submit a copy of such contract to the [Crime Victims B]oard and pay over to the [B]oard any moneys which would otherwise, by terms of such contract, be owing to the person so accused or convicted or his representatives.

"The Feds kept coming to me and saying: 'You're next, they are going to whack you. We could save your life,'" Hill later reported. With the prospect of a long prison term before him and fear that without protection from Vario, he could become Burke's latest target, Hill agreed to cooperate with federal authorities.

For the next several years, Hill, his wife, and their two children lived in hiding, their identity concealed under the federal witness protection program. The mob reportedly placed a $2 million price tag on his head. Guarded by federal marshals, Hill flew repeatedly to New York from his secret hideaway to testify in federal court. Over the course of seven years, Hill shared his knowledge of the intimate workings of the Mafia with judges, grand juries and trial court juries, and law enforcement officials. His testimony helped bring down mob bosses Vario, who received a ten-year sentence for extortion, and Burke, who was convicted of murder and of fixing Boston College basketball games. Both men died in prison, Vario at age seventy-three and Burke at age sixty-four. Hill also provided information that led to the conviction of at least thirty other members of organized crime families.

BOOK AND MOVIE DEALS

Hill's testimony and his reputation as an insider who knew the mob's secrets soon came to the attention of

Simon & Schuster, a major publisher with corporate offices in New York City. Executives at Simon & Schuster decided that Hill's story could be transformed into a profitable book. The publisher contacted literary agent Sterling Lord to find a writer who would work with Hill to produce a book on the mob based on Hill's revelations. Sterling contacted crime reporter Nicholas Pileggi, who readily agreed to write Hill's story. Pileggi had begun his career writing about organized crime for the Associated Press. Later, the well-respected journalist covered the same beat for *New York* magazine. Hill, too, signed on to the project.

On September 1, 1981, Hill and Pileggi signed contracts with Simon & Schuster to produce a nonfiction book on Hill's experiences. Both men received advance payments and promises of future royalties for their work once the book had been published. According to documents later filed with the court, Hill would not have participated in the project without payment.

The collaboration began as Hill was testifying against his former cronies. For the next two years, Hill told Pileggi his story during almost daily telephone calls. The author said Hill "had an outsider's eye for detail" that made his account especially revealing. The mobster "knew a great deal about the world in which he had been raised, but he spoke about it with an odd detachment," Pileggi noted. Hearing Hill describe mob life was "like talking to an aide-de-camp in Napoleon's headquarters. He knows how Napoleon likes his coffee." Hill, Pileggi realized, could pull back the curtains and expose the real people of the mob. "I wanted to know how these people lived," Pileggi said.

The author also met Hill in New York at prosecutors' offices and in various hotels, restaurants, and parks in the Midwest, where Hill lived under an alias. Witness protection program rules barred Pileggi from being given Hill's new name or his address. "We spent more than three hundred hours together [in person and on the telephone]; my notes of conversations with Henry occupy more than six linear file feet," Pileggi reported.

Wiseguy: Life in a Mafia Family, written by Pileggi but told mostly in Hill's words, came out in January 1986 to rave reviews. "Wiseguy," a term the mob used to describe a low-level Mafia hoodlum, referred to Hill, whose life, crimes, and involvement in the mob were the focus of the book. During his narrative, Hill admits that he took part "in an astonishing variety of crimes." At one point, he tells of the group's influence and control over New York's neighborhoods: When the gangsters entered a room, "the place stopped. Everyone knew who we were, and we were treated like movie stars with muscle."

Filled with detailed but unromanticized descriptions of the everyday lives of those in organized crime, the book became an instant best seller. Within nineteen

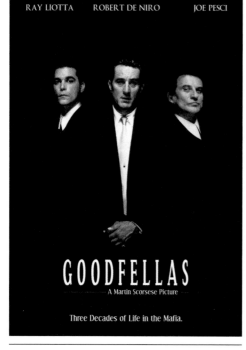

RAY LIOTTA   ROBERT DE NIRO   JOE PESCI

GOODFELLAS
A Martin Scorsese Picture

Three Decades of Life in the Mafia.

The film *GoodFellas*, based on Nicholas Pileggi's book *Wiseguy*, won acclaim after it was released in 1990.

months of publication, more than a million copies had been printed. The *New York Times*, among others, printed several glowing reviews of the book. *Times* book reviewer Christopher Lehmann-Haupt called the book *Wiseguy* "an irresistible oral history on organized crime in New York." Columnist Jimmy Breslin wrote in the *New York Daily News* that it was "the best book on crime in America ever written," and the *Washington Post* described it as an "entirely fascinating book that amounts to a piece of revisionist history."

The hoopla over the book put the spotlight on Hill again. In September 1986 the *New York Times* reported that he had been convicted six times for crimes ranging from driving without a license to burglary. Continuing coverage of Hill's testimony kept his name in the news as well.

Hill became even more well known when, in 1990, director Martin Scorsese based his movie *GoodFellas* on Pileggi's book and asked Pileggi to cowrite the screenplay. Scorsese, whose parents immigrated from Italy, said the book's honest portrayal of the mob's lifestyle attracted him: "It's time that we . . . really talk openly about this aspect of being Italian-American, not have it idealized, or mythologized, or shown as comedy. I'm just trying to show it straight—with all its attraction and all its horror." Joe Pesci won an Academy Award for best supporting actor in the film, which was also nominated in five other categories, including best picture and best screenwriter. The movie won acclaim from critics, receiving several awards from film organizations around the globe, and was later included in lists of the best pictures of all time.

Film critic Roger Ebert said of the movie, "No finer film has ever been made about organized crime—not even *The Godfather*." Like the book, the movie is narrated by Henry Hill (portrayed by Ray Liotta). It, too, offers a mesmerizing look inside the Mafia. Both the book and the movie netted millions in profits. Hill said in 2010 that he made $550,000 for his work on *GoodFellas* but claimed the film studio owed him millions more.

MONEY FOR VICTIMS

The splash created by *Wiseguy* did not go unnoticed by the members of the New York Crime Victims Board. On January 31, 1986, shortly after the book came out, the board directed Simon & Schuster to produce copies of any contracts with Henry Hill and an accounting of all payments made to the former mobster. The board also ordered the publisher to stop future payments to Hill.

Simon & Schuster complied. Its records showed that the company had paid $96,250 to Hill's literary agent on his behalf. An additional $27,958 in royalties had been earmarked for Hill but had not yet been paid. Upon receiving the notice from the Crime Victims Board, the publisher halted further payments to Hill.

After reviewing the documents and the book, the board ruled that Simon & Schuster and Hill had violated the state's Son of Sam law. On June 15, 1987, the board issued an order that all the money Hill earned for the project be turned over to the Crime Victims Board. Under the order, Simon & Schuster was required to pay the board all royalties being held for Hill, as well as any future payments. The board ordered Hill to turn over the funds he had already received for the project. If he failed to repay the money, Simon & Schuster would be required to make the payment, which the board noted should never have been paid to Hill.

This time the publisher refused to comply with the board's order. On August 3, 1987, Simon & Schuster filed suit against the Crime Victims Board in federal district court in New York City. The suit named the four members of the board, Gennaro Fischetti, George L. Grobe Jr., Diane McGrath, and Angelo Petromelis, as well as the board itself. Because the matter involved rights guaranteed by the U.S. Constitution, the case was heard in federal court.

In its brief, Simon & Schuster contended that New York's Son of Sam law violated the First Amendment by blocking the publication of certain books on crime. The suit noted that had the law been on the books in the past, it could have interfered with the publication of some of the nation's most important works, such as Henry David Thoreau's essay *Civil Disobedience* and *Letter from Birmingham Jail* by the Reverend Dr. Martin Luther King Jr. In his piece, Thoreau details his imprisonment for refusing to pay a poll tax, a fee that men in the 1800s had to pay in order to vote in some locales. Thoreau believed the tax was used to support slavery, which he bitterly opposed.

The essay—on the right and obligation of citizens to follow their own conscience—has been called "one of the most influential political tracts ever written by an American." *Letter from Birmingham Jail* describes King's actions in violation of local laws during a nonviolent protest against racial segregation in the South. The letter served as a rallying cry for civil rights activists intent on overturning such laws and ending racial discrimination in America.

In making their arguments, the lawyers laid heavy emphasis on their main contention: that the law

The Reverend Dr. Martin Luther King Jr. (*right*) and the Reverend Ralph Abernathy walk out of the Birmingham, Alabama, jail after being released in April 1963.

unconstitutionally interfered with freedom of the press and free-speech rights guaranteed by the First Amendment. Simon & Schuster also asserted that the statute was too broad and too vague, a violation of the Fourteenth Amendment's due process clause, which requires the government to follow fair regulations and procedures before depriving a citizen of life, liberty, or property. To be constitutional, therefore, state as well as national laws must be clear, fair, and reasonable.

In an opinion filed on October 26, 1989, district court judge John F. Keenan rejected the publisher's claims and upheld the New York law. The judge affirmed the board's order to confiscate Hill's royalties for the book and use them to compensate people who had been harmed by his crimes as detailed in *Wiseguy*. For example, merchants whose goods had been highjacked by Hill and his cronies could claim compensation for their losses. The state's law aimed to compensate crime victims, not to suppress free expression, Keenan ruled. Using the money from Hill's work to compensate victims "[did] not involve suppressing speech, but merely attaching the proceeds of that speech for the benefit of the victim." Any burden on free expression, he added, was merely "incidental." The law did not involve or infringe on political speech, he said, but "merely functions to prevent criminals from capitalizing on their crimes." Keenan also rejected the argument that the law was vague and too broad.

LIFE ON THE RUN

While the case against Simon & Schuster made its way through the court system, Henry Hill popped in and out of sight. During his years in hiding, Hill repeatedly blew his cover. A drug abuser and problem drinker, he was arrested several times for drug- and alcohol-related offenses, got involved with a number of women (he married one, but the marriage was annulled by his lawyers because he had not divorced his first wife), and informed strangers of his true identity while drunk. After moving the family from Nebraska to Kentucky to Washington State, the Justice Department finally threw the Hills out of the program. They continued to live in hiding for a while. In 1987 Hill's wife and children moved out, and Hill later remarried. The FBI paid Hill and provided him with some protection in return for additional information he supplied on the mob. He moved ten times and assumed as many aliases. He also continued to have problems with alcohol and drugs. In the early 1990s he began using his own name again, although he sometimes wore disguises in public.

CHAPTER TWO

FIRST AMENDMENT CHALLENGES

FOLLOWING NEW YORK'S LEAD, MANY OTHER states adopted their own Son of Sam laws. The statutes had a twin motive: to make sure criminals did not receive undue financial benefit from their crimes, and to ensure that the money criminals earned from descriptions of the crimes went to victims to compensate them for their losses. Most of the laws targeted criminals' assets earned from books or movies about their crimes. By the early 1990s forty-two states had Son of Sam laws on their books. In addition, Congress enacted the Victims of Crime Act of 1984, which made it easier for the government to seize crime-related assets, including proceeds from movies or books produced about the crimes committed.

Under such laws, publishers, movie producers, and

Crime victims and their supporters wear masks during a rally in New York City in 1997 to celebrate National Victims' Rights Week. The masks represent the need victims have to hide their suffering and shield themselves from society.

others who signed a contract with a criminal were required to submit a copy of the document and to turn over to a state crime victims board any income due the criminal under the terms of the contract. As in New York, the money would then be placed in an escrow account for victims of the crime. In most states, victims had to sue a criminal in civil court and win a judgment for damages in order to collect the money. A few laws allowed victims to apply directly to the state for compensation from the fund. In most cases, victims had from three to five years to collect the proceeds. Some states returned the money to the criminal if no one applied for it. Others kept the money in the fund and turned it over to a court to allocate.

Money left in state funds could eventually be deposited in the Federal Crime Victims Fund, which provides services for victims nationwide. In addition to forfeited profits, the fund receives revenue from criminals' fines, forfeited bonds, assessments, and donations. Among its many services, the national fund helps pay for medical costs, funeral and burial costs, lost wages, and counseling for those victimized by criminals. A portion of the money in the federal fund went to assist victims and survivors of victims of the terrorist attacks of September 11, 2001.

THE JEAN HARRIS CASE

Henry Hill was not the only criminal to challenge New York's Son of Sam law. Jean Harris filed a similar suit in state court after the New York Crime Victims Board confiscated royalties from her autobiography, *Stranger in Two Worlds*. On March 10, 1980, Harris, the headmistress of an exclusive girls' school in McLean, Virginia, shot and killed her longtime lover, Herman Tarnower, a physician and best-selling author who gained fame as the "Scarsdale diet doctor." A jury convicted her of second-degree murder, and the judge ordered a sentence of fifteen years to life in prison. While serving her prison term, Harris wrote the book about her life. She said in

Jean Harris poses for a photograph in 1983 while serving time for the murder of her lover, Dr. Herman Tarnower.

the autobiography that she had intended to kill herself, not Tarnower, and that the gun had gone off accidentally. Macmillan Publishers released the book in June 1986 and paid royalties to Harris. Because of Harris's notoriety and the publicity her case received, *Stranger in Two Worlds* promised to be a big seller.

Harris received around $100,000 for writing the

book. She planned to donate the money to a nonprofit organization dedicated to helping the children of prisoners. New York State intervened, saying that Harris's profits had to be set aside for the survivors of the victim of her crime under the Son of Sam law.

Lawyers for Harris and the New York Civil Liberties Union sued. They claimed that the law violated the free-speech guarantee in the First Amendment. If the court allowed the law to stand, the lawyers argued, it would have a chilling effect on speech related to crimes.

The case went all the way to the New York Court of Appeals, the state's highest court. It became the first Son of Sam suit to be heard by that court. In a 5-to-0 ruling, delivered on May 8, 1991, the court upheld the law and rejected Harris's claims. The decision, written by Judge Richard D. Simons, found that New York's law did not jeopardize criminals' right to speak or write about their crimes; it merely barred them from getting paid for doing so. The law, the judge wrote, supported the "equitable principle that criminals should not be permitted to profit from their wrongs."

Judge Simons said that there would never have been a market for books and movies covered by the law without the criminals' commission of crimes. These criminals "had no marketable asset before the crime," the judge noted. "They create, by illegal activity, a new product—a story—which becomes profitable in the retelling."

CONFISCATING PROFITS FROM CRIME STORIES

At the time of the Harris decision, the New York law had been used in nine other cases to confiscate royalties of criminals, including Henry Hill. Among those blocked from receiving funds from books or movies about their crimes were Mark David Chapman, who murdered singer John Lennon in New York City in 1980, and Jack Henry Abbott, another murderer, who wrote the best seller *In the Belly of the Beast*, a collection of letters about his life in prison, addressed to his famous mentor, author Norman Mailer. As a result of efforts by Mailer and others, Abbott had been released on parole. The day before the *New York Times* reviewed his book, however, he

Barbara Walters interviewed Mark David Chapman in 2000 at Attica Correctional Facility in New York, where he is serving twenty years to life in prison for the murder of rock musician John Lennon.

stabbed a young actor to death. A court froze the assets from the book, and a jury in a civil suit later awarded them to the actor's widow. In another case, a lower court ordered the return of royalties earned by Sydney Biddle Barrows for her book *Mayflower Madam*, an account of her operation of a prostitution ring. The judge in the case ruled that prostitution was a crime without victims and therefore did not fall under the law's regulations.

In all, victims who made claims under New York's Son of Sam law received only about $71,450 from the state fund—all seized from John Wojtowicz, the bank robber whose exploits served as the plot for the film *Dog Day Afternoon*. Other money remained in escrow, including Harris's and Hill's royalties. Only one victim applied to collect Hill's royalties, according to Hill's lawyer.

TAKING THE PROFIT OUT OF CRIME

Governments have long held that criminals should not benefit from their crimes. An early case affirmed the premise. In 1889 the New York state court ruled that a sixteen-year-old boy who had killed his grandfather could not inherit the older man's estate. The decision asserted that "no one shall be permitted to profit by his own fraud, or to take advantage of his own wrong, or to found any claim upon his own iniquity, or to acquire property by his own crime." This was confirmed in 1972, in the decision in *Petrie v. Chase Manhattan Bank*.

Here the appellate division of the New York Supreme Court had ordered that a woman forfeit the estate of a man killed by her brother. The court determined that the killer had exerted undue influence on the man to name his sister in the will. In reaching the decision, the court noted, "It is indisputable law that a murderer cannot profit from his felonious act by inheriting from his victim . . . or by any other means."

Most states had statutes that allowed the government to seize assets a criminal gained through the commission of a crime. In 1989 the U.S. Supreme Court upheld a federal law that authorized the forfeiture of all property derived from illegal drug operations. Justice Byron White delivered the decision in the case, *Caplin & Drysdale, Chartered v. United States.* The ruling allowed the forfeiture of all drug-related funds, including the money the defendant had paid his lawyers to represent him. "Forfeiture provisions are powerful weapons in the war on crime," Justice White wrote.

Likewise, both state and federal governments embraced the concept that criminals should compensate the victims of their crimes. In fact, money from the federal Victims of Crime Act of 1984 was earmarked to assist victims and to help fund victim compensation programs operating in thirty-five states.

Although almost everyone applauded the effort to use criminals' money to compensate their victims, not everyone supported the Son of Sam laws' focus on assets derived from speech-related activities. Publicity surrounding high-profile cases such as those of David Berkowitz and Henry Hill convinced lawmakers that books and movies about criminals would produce the largest source of funds. Most criminals, however, attracted little interest from publishers or film producers, so the law applied only in a limited number of cases.

CONSTITUTIONAL CONCERNS

The seizure of funds derived from speech-related projects raised a red flag for legal experts concerned with protecting constitutional rights. American democracy relies on the First Amendment's guarantees of free speech and freedom of the press. People need the information provided by publishers and the media in order to function knowledgeably as citizens. If officials had the power to ban words and speech they did not like and proceeded to misuse this power, Americans would not have enough information to decide for themselves whether the words had merit.

Even in the case of the Son of Sam laws, which have the admirable goals of compensating victims for their injuries and preventing criminals from profiting from their crimes, the result can prevent citizens from learning valuable information. A criminal's book might reveal corruption in government, failures in the social welfare system, or unacceptable conditions in prisons—all issues that people who read about them might be motivated to address. But if criminals received no payment for telling their story, they might choose to remain silent, and many potentially useful discussions would never take place. That was one point that Simon & Schuster's lawyers would make during the publisher's appeal of the Henry Hill matter.

While the Harris case was being heard in the state courts, Simon & Schuster's litigation followed a different route in the federal court system. After the district court's decision against its claims, the publisher appealed to the U.S. Court of Appeals. Three nonprofit organizations—PEN American Center (a group of poets, playwrights, essayists, editors, and novelists), the New York Civil Liberties Union, and the Association of American Publishers—filed briefs in support of the publisher. These *amicus curiae* (or "friend of the court") briefs presented the groups' arguments that the New York law violated the First Amendment.

NEAR V. MINNESOTA: *DON'T STOP THE PRESSES*

Lawyers for Simon & Schuster argued their appeal on March 22, 1990. They relied on several previous Supreme Court decisions to support their case. Perhaps the most important was *Near v. Minnesota*, the Supreme Court's first major ruling to protect the freedom of the press. The decision, issued in 1931, put severe limits on the government's ability to control the American press.

The case involved a newspaper's scandalous accounts of crimes committed by "Jewish gangsters" in Minneapolis. The crimes were detailed in a series charging that the gangs ran gambling, bootlegging, and racketeering operations. The articles, which were published in *The Saturday Press* in 1927, also denounced local officials for assisting in the crimes or turning a blind eye to the illegal activity. County attorney Floyd B. Olson, who had been a target of *The Saturday Press*'s accusations, sued Jay M. Near, the newspaper's publisher, and asked the court to stop further publication of the articles. The Minnesota law on which Olson based his suit banned publication of "a malicious, scandalous and defamatory newspaper, magazine or other periodical" as a public nuisance. If certain articles were challenged under the law, a publisher could continue to print them only by proving the material was true and published "with good motives and for justifiable ends."

The district court ruled that the newspaper had indeed published "malicious, scandalous, and defamatory" articles and shut the paper down. Near appealed to the state supreme court. He argued that the state law violated both the First Amendment's guarantee of freedom of the press and the Fourteenth Amendment, which forbids states from depriving citizens of their liberties without due process of law. In a unanimous opinion, the Minnesota court upheld the law and rejected Near's claims.

The publisher appealed to the U.S. Supreme Court, which ruled 5-to-4 in Near's favor. Writing for the majority in the landmark decision, Chief Justice Charles Evans Hughes declared that it was almost always unconstitutional to put restraints on publication. Under the Constitution, Hughes wrote, except in very rare circumstances, the presses can't be stopped—not by courts, not even by public officials who have reason to believe that the material to be printed will target them unjustly.

Americans and their courts held a "deep-seated conviction that such restraints would violate constitutional right," the Court's leader wrote. The "chief purpose" of the First Amendment's guarantee of press freedom, he said, was "to prevent previous restraints upon publication." Libel laws were in place to punish those who published false, scandalous material, Hughes noted. Putting prior restraints on publication—even by irresponsible publishers—would threaten the very underpinning of a free nation.

"The fact that the liberty of the press may be abused by miscreant purveyors of scandal does not make any the less necessary the immunity of the press from previous restraint in dealing with official misconduct," the chief justice wrote.

Chief Justice Charles Evans Hughes wrote a landmark decision in 1931 in the case *Near v. Minnesota*. The decision established that it was almost always unconstitutional for the government to stop the presses.

The decision also attacked a provision in the Minnesota law, which required a publisher to prove ahead of time that his statements were true and that he was printing the material "with good motives." To do so, a publisher would be forced to get approval to publish from officials, some of whom might be the targets of the articles under dispute. If this were allowed, Hughes noted, officials could deny publication of material they disagreed with, and "it would be but a step to a complete system of censorship."

The press could be restrained in a few exceptional cases, Hughes said: during wartime, for example, the government could stop publications that interfered with recruitment or revealed national secrets like sailing dates of ships or the number and location of troops. America owed its independence and freedoms, in large part, to the free press, Hughes noted. "To the press alone, chequered as it is with abuses, the world is indebted for all the triumphs which have been gained by reason and humanity over error and oppression."

MEYER V. GRANT: "STRICT SCRUTINY" TEST

In their appeal, coming sixty years after *Near*, the lawyers for Simon & Schuster also relied heavily on a more recent decision, issued in 1988 in the case of *Meyer v. Grant*. The Court had established in 1919 that speech that presents a "clear and present danger" to society can be banned. In the *Meyer* ruling, the justices decreed that government must use a "strict scrutiny" test before limiting speech that does not present such danger. The "strict scrutiny" test requires the government to prove that its restrictions "promote a compelling interest" and are "the least restrictive means" to further that interest.

In its decision in the *Meyer* case, the Court ruled that the state's compelling interest did not outweigh the free-speech rights of the plaintiff. The decision struck down a Colorado law that made it a felony to pay people to circulate petitions in referendum drives. The law also required that those who circulated petitions had to be registered voters in the state, a provision that was also voided. The case involved a group called Coloradans for Free Enterprise, which wanted to hire workers to collect signatures for a ballot initiative its members supported. The group asked the district court to lift the law's restrictions on hiring people who were not registered Colorado voters to collect signatures on petitions.

The state of Colorado argued that the law helped prevent fraud. It also asserted that the law ensured that successful petition drives reflected widespread support for an issue, not manipulation of the process by wealthy special interests. The district court upheld the law, but a federal court of appeals overturned it on the grounds that it interfered with "core political speech" protected under the First Amendment. The state appealed to the Supreme Court, which upheld the appeals court's decision and ruled the Colorado law unconstitutional.

In writing for the unanimous Court, Justice John Paul Stevens said of the First Amendment that it "was fashioned to assure unfettered interchange of ideas for the bringing about of political and social changes desired by the people." The law banning paid circulators, Justice Stevens declared, restricted political expression and must therefore be "subject to exacting scrutiny." Since that was the case, "the burden that Colorado must overcome to justify this criminal law is well nigh insurmountable." The fact that group members could still express their political views in some ways (using volunteers to circulate petitions, for example) did not mean the state could put limits on other types of political expression. Whether the government ordered a total ban or a partial ban on a First Amendment right, it had to prove an overriding interest that justified any infringement of a fundamental right and prove that the government's interest could not be met in any other way. In this case, the Court ruled, the state failed to meet that burden. Justice Stevens concluded that the state did not have to interfere with First Amendment rights in order to meet its objectives.

The lawyers for Simon & Schuster cited the *Meyer* decision in their appeal. They argued that the state of New York did not meet the strict scrutiny test. The Son of Sam law, they observed, restricted speech based on its content, yet the content itself did not pose a danger. The state's "compelling interests" of making sure crime did not pay and of reimbursing crime victims, the lawyers contended, could be accomplished through other means and did not trump their client's free-speech rights.

CHAPTER THREE

LOWER COURTS UPHOLD THE LAW

ON OCTOBER 3, 1990, THE APPEALS COURT, BY A vote of 2-to-1, upheld New York's Son of Sam law. It disagreed with the lower court's reasoning but supported the law for different reasons. Unlike the lower court, the appeals panel ruled that the law did indeed place direct restrictions on a criminal's speech. "Without a financial incentive to relate their criminal activities, most would-be storytellers will decline to speak or write," declared Judge Roger J. Miner in his majority opinion. The appeals court also noted that the First Amendment protects all types of speech, not just that involving political matters: "Protected expression comes in many forms."

The appeals court also determined that the law indeed restricted criminals' speech or other expression based on its content. Under the law, for example, a convict could collect payments for writing a cookbook but not for a book that mentioned the crimes he or she committed. Because the law restricted speech, the state had to prove that the interests promoted by the law were compelling enough to override a basic right. Two of the three judges agreed, however, that the state's interest in preventing criminals from profiting from their crimes—and helping ensure that their victims were compensated for the harm caused them—was a strong enough reason to allow an infringement of free-speech rights. "Our society rightly deems it fundamentally unfair for a criminal to be paid for recounting the story of his or her crime while the victim remains uncompensated for financial loss occasioned by the crime," wrote Judge Miner.

Simon & Schuster had argued that the state's laws allowed the courts to order payment to victims who won damages from criminals. The appeals court, however, asserted that the current laws had limits and did not apply in certain victims' cases. The only asset most criminals had, Judge Miner wrote, was "the right to tell the story of their crimes." New York's law did not prevent criminals from talking or writing about their crimes, he said. It merely prohibited criminals from getting paid for such speech.

The Son of Sam law had other purposes as well, the judge noted. It lessened the burden on society to pay for victims' treatment, provided victims with a "sense of justice and . . . retribution," and made criminals more aware of the consequences of their crimes. Because of the important goals the law sought to achieve, the court said, it met the "strict scrutiny" standard set forth in the *Meyer* ruling. Thus the court agreed that the law could be used to override Henry Hill's right to free speech.

Judge Jon Ormond Newman disagreed. In his dissent, he argued that the state's interests, while admirable, did not outweigh Hill's fundamental rights, nor did its provisions meet the "strict scrutiny" test. He believed that in their zeal to protect crime victims and to keep the perpetrators from profiting, legislators had passed a law that violated the First Amendment. By upholding the statute, Newman said, the court impaired protections guaranteed by the Constitution and deprived the public "of valuable writings about activities of high public interest."

Newman said the state law applied only to profits derived from speech about specific topics, not to other types of payments received by criminals. He cited the Jean Harris case as an example. Her book focused on prison conditions, but because two chapters referred to her crime, the Crime Victims Board ordered Harris's royalties from the book to be diverted to the escrow fund for victims. If Harris had not included the two chapters, Newman said, the royalties would have gone to her for distribution to her charitable fund. Furthermore, he disagreed with his fellow judges' claim that selling their

IN THE WORDS OF HENRY HILL

Henry Hill's words fill much of the 360 pages of *Wiseguy* by Nicholas Pileggi. The mob underling, who spent more than three hundred hours discussing his life in organized crime with Pileggi, begins his account with his introduction, at age eleven, to the mobsters at the cab stand across the street from his childhood home in Brooklyn, New York. During the next year, he became official errand boy for the mob members who ran the stand. "At the age of twelve my ambition was to be a gangster. To be a wiseguy," Hill relates. "To me being a wiseguy was better than being president of the United States."

He tells of skipping school to make pickups for the mob. The young boy received a beating from his father after the truant officer sent a notice to Hill's parents about his frequent absences from school. When Hill complained to his gangster friends, they threatened the mailman, who stopped delivering the school's mail to Henry's parents.

By his twenties, Hill was a full-fledged associate of the mob, with all the jewels, cash, and other perks that came with the job. "Truckloads of swag. Fur coats, televisions, clothes—all for the asking," he says of his life back then. "When I was broke I just went out and robbed some more. We ran everything. We paid the lawyers. We paid the cops. Everybody had their hands out. We walked out laughing. We had the best of everything."

Nicholas Pileggi based his bestselling book *Wiseguy* on Henry Hill's accounts of his life as an underling with the mob.

Lawlessness was central to existence. He recalls attacking restaurant workers on behalf of mob boss Paul Vario, who had been enraged at the way the staff had treated him. "I never saw Paulie so angry. . . . Within an hour we had two carloads of guys with baseball bats and pipes waiting outside Don Pepe's [restaurant]. We were chasing waiters and breaking heads all over Brooklyn that night. It was so easy. Lump them up. Whack them out. Nobody ever thought, Why? What for?"

story was the only asset most criminals possessed. He contended that not all criminals were poor, that many had assets of their own, and that most criminals did not have a story like Hill's worth selling.

To meet the strict scrutiny test, the judge said, lawmakers had to show that the state's worthy goals could be met only by infringing on a criminal's rights. In New York State, he said, victims could have received compensation from other assets owned by a criminal, not just those derived from books and movies about the crime.

Newman said the law could not be justified by the fact that people would be outraged if criminals benefited from writing or speaking about their crimes. He cited several cases in which the Supreme Court had ruled that First Amendment rights could not be restricted merely in response to public outrage. For example, in *Hustler v. Falwell* the high court rejected minister Jerry Falwell's claim of damages for a scurrilous and outrageous parody published in the men's magazine. And, he noted, if no qualified person sued for the money within the required time period, victims' rights supporters presumably still would be outraged by the fact that the law allowed a criminal to collect royalties from his story of crime.

Additionally, the law applied to those only accused of a crime as well as those already convicted. A person found not guilty could reclaim the royalties, but the law might well deter publishers from giving an advance to anyone who faced a trial. As a practical matter, such deterrence was likely, since publishers would have to hand over a criminal's advance if he or she did not repay it to the board. "It is clear," Newman said, "that the prohibition of such advances will deter the writing of books by many innocent persons falsely accused of crime."

The law also encouraged publishers to censor material they suspected might fall under the Son of Sam law, including even brief mentions of a criminal's "thoughts, feelings, opinions, or emotions" about the crime. "Such governmentally induced suppression of speech is anathema to the First Amendment," Newman said.

He concluded that not only did the law interfere with protected speech, it also failed to meet its goals of compensating victims. In the eleven years since the law was enacted, Newman said, only five escrow accounts—three with money from the same person—had been established to aid victims. Other state laws allowed victims to sue criminals for damages and collect royalties.

The law, the judge said, reduced the money available to victims by discouraging the publication of criminals' books. He ended his opinion with a quotation from the Supreme Court's ruling in *Regan v. Time*, delivered in 1984: "Regulations which permit the Government to discriminate on the basis of the content of the message cannot be tolerated under the First Amendment." The lawyers for Simon & Schuster would use the judge's dissent in presenting their case to the Supreme Court.

ARKANSAS WRITERS' PROJECT: TAX UNFAIR

Another recent Court decision, in *Arkansas Writers' Project, Inc. v. Ragland*, would also play a role in the *Simon & Schuster* case. The *Arkansas Writers' Project* ruling, issued in 1987, established strict rules for states that sought to put restrictions on First Amendment rights. To justify a regulation that infringed on the First Amendment, the Court ruled, a state must have a "compelling" interest that can be served only by the legislation. The Court also required that states enact a "narrowly drawn" law that applied only to the compelling interest. The decision reaffirmed the Court's earlier ruling that the First Amendment does not allow government officials to single out publications based on their content.

Justice Thurgood Marshall delivered the opinion for the Court on April 22, 1987. By a 7-to-2 vote, the Court struck down an Arkansas law that taxed certain publications but exempted others. The state required customers to pay a sales tax on magazines of general interest, which covered a variety of topics. The tax did not apply to newspapers or to religious, professional, trade, and sports journals, which targeted various specific audiences.

The Arkansas Writers' Project, which published a general-interest magazine in the state, filed suit against Charles D. Ragland, Arkansas revenue commissioner, in 1984. The publishing company contended that the tax system discriminated against its magazine and infringed on freedom of the press. The firm sought a refund of sales taxes paid since 1982. The state argued that the sales tax was "an ordinary form of taxation," which the Court, in previous rulings, had allowed to be applied to publishers as well as anyone else. When the magazine's claims were rejected in the lower courts, the publisher took the case to the Supreme Court.

Justice Thurgood Marshall wrote the majority opinion in the Arkansas tax case cited in the Son of Sam litigation.

Justice Marshall first rejected the tax law's content-based criteria. The Arkansas tax was discriminatory because it applied to only a few publications and clearly "burdens rights protected by the First Amendment." The law was "particularly repugnant," the justice said, because a magazine's tax status depended entirely on its content. To determine whether a publication qualified for a tax exemption, officials had to examine its articles. Marshall wrote: "Such official scrutiny of the content of publications as the basis for imposing a tax is entirely incompatible with the First Amendment's guarantee of freedom of the press." Quoting from an earlier case, he declared: "[A]bove all else, the First Amendment means that government has no power to restrict expression because of its message, its ideas, its subject matter, or its content."

Because the law infringed on a right guaranteed by the First Amendment, the Court required the state to have "compelling" reasons for the need for that infringement: "In order to justify such differential taxation, the State must show that its regulation is necessary to serve a compelling state interest, and is narrowly drawn to achieve that end." The state justified the law on the grounds that it raised needed revenue, while providing exemptions to newspapers, which reported current events, and to journals, in order to encourage "fledgling" publishers.

The Court ruled that Arkansas's reasons failed to meet the "heavy burden" required. The goal of the law—to raise money—could have been accomplished by taxing all publications equally, Marshall said. Furthermore, the law was too broad. Its exemption of religious, professional, trade, and sports journals benefited far more than just small publications, and "fledgling" general interest magazines did not qualify for the law's exemption.

Two earlier cases, *United States v. O'Brien* in 1968 and *Shapiro v. Thompson* in 1969, had made virtually the same point: that a state law restricting a fundamental right had to be "essential" to promote "a compelling government interest," and it had to be targeted narrowly on that aim.

CHAPTER FOUR

TO THE SUPREME COURT

UNDETERRED BY THE COURT OF APPEALS ruling, Simon & Schuster's lawyers decided to appeal the case to the next level: the U.S. Supreme Court. The high court receives requests for hearings from more than nine thousand petitioners each year and rules on fewer than one hundred of those cases. To win a spot on the docket, a case must involve issues of national importance. Cases qualifying for review by the Supreme Court must fall into one of three categories: constitutional rights or questions, conflicts between rulings of different courts, or rulings by state courts on a federal law. The Supreme Court also considers cases involving ambassadors, consuls, and foreign ministers.

As the highest court in the land, the U.S. Supreme Court rules on cases that will set standards of law for the nation. Judges in lower courts use Supreme Court decisions to guide them when they issue their own rulings.

Lawyers usually file a petition with the Court requesting that their case be heard. This petition for a writ of *certiorari* outlines the reasons the Court should consider the case. *Certiorari* means "to be more fully informed." The Court denies most such petitions, and the decisions of lower courts remain in force. If the Court does grant *certiorari*, the records of the case are transferred from the lower courts to the Supreme Court, so that the justices will be "fully informed" of the proceedings. Usually the chief justice selects cases he believes are important and submits the list to the associate justices during a private conference. The eight associates review the list and discuss their views on whether cases should be scheduled for a hearing. To be selected, a case must get the votes of at least four of the nine justices. Associate justices can also present cases they believe the Court should hear. Although it can take several years for a case to reach the high court, in matters of extreme urgency—for example a national emergency—the Court can agree to hear a case without delay.

The Court conducts no trial, instructs no jury, and hears no testimony. Instead, the justices rely on the records of the lower courts' proceedings; the opposing lawyers' briefs, in which both sides lay out their arguments and cite relevant previous rulings; and oral arguments, during

Activist Abbie Hoffman during a political protest in 1969. Simon & Schuster's lawyers claimed the New York Son of Sam law would have discouraged the publishing of Hoffman's memoirs because of his criminal record.

which the lawyers briefly plead their case and answer the justices' questions.

In making their case for a hearing, Simon & Schuster's lawyers contended that New York's Son of Sam law violated the First Amendment guarantee of freedom of expression. The law deterred publishers from printing newsworthy and other valuable material, they said. They noted that the law, had it been in effect earlier, could have discouraged the publishing of a number of well-respected books, citing among them *Witness*, Whittaker Chambers's acclaimed account of his testimony in the spy trial of Alger Hiss, and the memoirs of Abbie Hoffman, a political dissident of the 1960s. "Review is urgently warranted," Simon & Schuster told the Court in its petition. Until the case was reviewed and the law overturned, the publisher said, there would be "repeated . . . decisions by authors not to create, and by publishers not to commission and publish, works of substantial social value."

The Association of American Publishers (AAP) and the Motion Picture Association of America (MPAA) filed separate briefs in support of Simon & Schuster's appeal. The AAP argued that "crime has always been a subject of public interest and fascination, and writings about crime are a staple of our literary heritage." If the law were left in place, the association contended, it would "contract that debate, to society's detriment, by limiting the creation of works dealing with crime."

In its brief, the film association said that Son of Sam laws were "an impediment" to filmmakers who wanted to produce cinematic works on important subjects. As an example, the association cited a potential film on Willie Horton, a convict who committed rape, robbery, and assault while on an officially approved temporary leave from prison. Presidential candidate George H. W. Bush used Horton's story to his advantage in advertisements during the campaign in 1988. "In the wake of the most recent presidential election, if a filmmaker decides to film the Willie Horton story and the filmmaker determines that Willie Horton is a crucial source and Horton demands payment before he will cooperate, should the

IS THIS YOUR PRO-FAMILY

TEAM FOR 1988 ?

DUKAKIS

HORTON

Dear Fellow Marylander:

By now, you have heard of the Dukakis/Bentsen team.

But have you heard of the Dukakis/Willie Horton team?

This is the real team which voters, in particular pro-family voters, should be concerned about because it's the Dukakis/Willie Horton team which really tells what you can expect if Mike Dukakis is elected in November.

You see, Willie Horton is the Massachusetts killer Dukakis released as part of his prison furlough program for first degree murderers sentenced to life without parole. Like fifty-eight of his fellow killers, he decided not to return to prison when his weekend of fun was over.

Like many of his fellow escapees, Horton committed further violent crimes while on his "extended" furlough. In Horton's case, he came to Maryland to ply his trade.

The Dukakis/Horton story began on the night of October 26, 1974 when Horton robbed a gas station in Massachusetts. Horton, on parole at the time for assault with intent to murder, wasn't satisfied with merely robbing the 17 year-old station operator. So, he stabbed the boy 19 times, stuffed him into a trash can and left the boy to die.

Horton was captured and convicted of armed robbery and first-degree murder in May of 1975. Unfortunately for honest citizens, Massachusetts' new governor Mike Dukakis had, several weeks earlier, vetoed the death penalty bill in Massachusetts. Horton was sentenced to life imprisonment without parole.

Thus was the Dukakis/Horton team born.

By 1986, Horton was receiving weekend furloughs from Dukakis. After one of his "weekend vacations" Horton, surprisingly enough, failed to return to custody.

Horton was able to run as a direct result of his teammate Mike Dukakis' actions. You see, in 1975 the Massachusetts'

(Over, please)

Paid for by Maryland Republican Party. Contributions are not deductible for federal income tax purposes.

A copy of the letter sent by the Maryland Republican Party using the story of Willie Horton to win votes for GOP presidential candidate George H. W. Bush in 1988.

government be allowed to erect an impediment to the filmmakers' decision to use Horton?" the MPAA asked in the brief it submitted to the Court.

The state of New York, represented by Robert Abrams, its attorney general, asked the Court to reject Simon & Schuster's request for appeal. Abrams noted that the law protected "profits for the sake of victims," but he argued that it did not "prohibit a criminal from speaking about his crime, nor does it prohibit a publisher from publishing the criminal's reenactment or discussion of the crime." The statute, he said, took aim "only at the money to be paid the criminal and not at his expression."

On February 19, 1991, the Supreme Court informed Simon & Schuster that the justices would consider the case, now titled *Simon & Schuster v. Members of the New York State Crime Victims Board*. Each side would file briefs with the Court, and oral arguments would be heard on October 15, 1991.

THE BRIEFS

The *Simon & Schuster* case attracted forty-one briefs, all submitted to the Court for review. Attorneys Charles S. Sims, Mark C. Morril, and Ronald S. Rauchberg filed the brief detailing the publisher's arguments. Attorney General Abrams, Solicitor General O. Peter Sherwood, and Howard L. Zwickel and Susan L. Watson, both assistant attorneys general, prepared New York's brief.

The brief filed on behalf of the publisher recapped many of the arguments presented to the appeals court. In addition to *Meyer v. Grant* and several others, two flag-burning cases strengthened the publisher's position. In its rulings in *Texas v. Johnson*, issued in 1989, and *U.S. v. Eichman*, issued in 1990, the Supreme Court confirmed that even offensive speech (or an offensive expressive act, like burning a flag) was protected under the First Amendment. Both decisions, on narrow 5-to-4 votes, gave protesters the right to burn American flags as a way of expressing opposition to government policy.

Justice William J. Brennan Jr., writing the majority opinion in *Texas v. Johnson*, affirmed that actions that expressed political views were protected under the First Amendment even if they offended onlookers: "If there is a bedrock principle underlying the First Amendment, it is that the Government may not prohibit the expression of an idea simply because society finds the idea itself offensive or disagreeable." He also noted that the state of Texas had penalized Johnson's political expression "because of the content of the message he conveyed." Because the state law infringed on a fundamental right—free expression—the state's interest in banning flag burning had to meet "the most exacting scrutiny." That, the Court ruled, the state had failed to do.

In the second flag-burning case, *U.S. v. Eichman*, the Court struck down a law enacted by Congress that made it a crime for protesters to burn the American flag. Justice Brennan again wrote the opinion for the Court, using many of the same arguments expressed in *Texas*

Police restrain a protester after he set fire to an American flag on the steps of the Supreme Court. The Court later ruled that burning the flag as a political protest is protected by the First Amendment.

v. Johnson. The law violated the First Amendment because "its asserted interest" was "related to the suppression of free expression and concerned with the content of such expression," Brennan wrote.

Thirty-nine entities submitted *amicus curiae* briefs. Three organizations—the AAP, the MPAA, and the American Civil Liberties Union—filed briefs supporting Simon & Schuster's call to repeal the law. Thirty-four states with legislation similar to New York's Son of Sam law and the nonpartisan Council of State Governments submitted briefs asking that the law be retained. In a separate brief in support of the federal Victims of Crime Act, the U.S. Justice Department argued that, unlike New York's legislation, the 1984 law was "narrowly tailored" to meet its goal: it targeted assets only from people convicted of a federal crime.

THE JUSTICES

Only eight Supreme Court justices participated in the *Simon & Schuster* case. In anticipation of the retirement of Justice Thurgood Marshall, scheduled for October 1991, President George H. W. Bush had nominated Clarence Thomas to fill the upcoming vacancy. Because of charges of sexual harassment against him and controversies over Thomas's qualifications, however, Senate hearings on his confirmation extended over three months. The Senate confirmed Thomas on October 15, but the new associate justice was not sworn in until October 23, eight days after the presentation of oral arguments in *Simon & Schuster v. Members of the New York State Crime Victims Board.*

Chief Justice William Rehnquist headed the Court that would rule on the case. Nominated as an associate justice by President Richard Nixon in 1971, Rehnquist had joined the Court in 1972. In 1986 President Ronald Reagan nominated him to fill the chief justice post after the incumbent, Warren Burger, retired. Rehnquist, who had been a deputy attorney general in the Nixon administration before his appointment as a justice, was widely recognized as the leader of the conservative wing of the Court. More than any other justice on the Court at the time, he sided with the government over the press or individuals in free-speech cases. Dissenting from the majority of the Court, Rehnquist had voted to uphold laws that, among other things, punished flag burners, restricted the display and content of political signs, and barred advertisements for abortion clinics.

The seven associate justices who voted on the *Simon & Schuster* case were:

• Byron R. White, nominated by President John F. Kennedy in 1962. White, at the time of this case the longest-serving member on the Rehnquist Court, was a former professional football player and a Rhodes scholar who had briefly served as deputy U.S. attorney general in Kennedy's administration. He often played a centrist role on the Court. His votes on First Amendment issues were mixed, and the press did not consider him a friend to their cause. White voted with the majority in *New York Times v. Sullivan*, which eased libel laws for the press, but he later changed his views on the ruling. He generally believed that the First Amendment did not necessarily guarantee the press special treatment.

• Harry A. Blackmun, nominated by President Nixon in 1970. He became most noted for his majority opinion in the 1973 case *Roe v. Wade*, on a woman's right to abortion. Blackmun made his most important contribution to free speech in three opinions that extended First Amendment protections to commercial speech. The cases, all decided in the 1970s, struck down state laws that barred abortion clinics, pharmacists, and lawyers from advertising their services. Although

Blackmun gradually emerged as a member of the liberal wing of the Court, he did not always cast his vote for freedom of expression. In 1988 Blackmun joined with White and Rehnquist in dissenting from a ruling, in *Boos v. Barry*, that upheld the First Amendment right of protesters to display political signs.

• John Paul Stevens, nominated by President Gerald R. Ford in 1975. Stevens was considered a moderate, though independent-minded, voice on the Court. During World War II he was part of a code-breaking team for the navy. In practicing law before being appointed to the U.S. Court of Appeals, Stevens had specialized in antitrust cases. As a judge, he had a mixed record on free-speech issues, opposing First Amendment protections for pornography and flag burners but supporting the right of protesters to display political signs.

• Sandra Day O'Connor, the first woman to serve on the Court, nominated by President Ronald Reagan in 1981. In her first six years on the bench, O'Connor tended to side with conservative justices on the issues of free speech and freedom of the press, but in 1988 she wrote the majority opinion in *Boos v. Barry*, involving protesters who wished to picket the embassies of the Soviet Union and Nicaragua in Washington, D.C.

The Court ruled that the law's restrictions against displaying political signs violated the First Amendment.

• Antonin G. Scalia, nominated in 1986 by President Reagan. Though he usually voted with the Court's most conservative members, Scalia emerged in several cases as an advocate of free speech. He voted with the majority in *Texas v. Johnson* and *U.S. v. Eichman* to overturn laws banning flag burning as a means of political expression. Scalia also voted with the majority in *Boos v. Barry*.

• Anthony M. Kennedy, nominated in 1988 by President Reagan. Kennedy took over his father's law practice and later was appointed as a judge on the U.S. Court of Appeals. He became a swing vote on the Supreme Court. A conservative on crime and other issues, Kennedy assumed the role of chief advocate for free speech after the retirement of Justice Brennan. In the flag-burning cases, he joined Justice Scalia as well as the liberal members of the Court to strike down laws that banned such acts of political expression. In a short concurrence to Brennan's opinion in the Texas case, Kennedy wrote: "The hard fact is that sometimes we must make decisions we do not like. We make them because they are right, right in the sense that the law and the Constitution, as we see them, compel the result." He later would uphold the free-speech rights of individuals against government in almost 75 percent of the First Amendment cases before the Court.

• David H. Souter, nominated to the Court in 1990 by President George H. W. Bush. A Rhodes scholar and former New Hampshire attorney general, Souter was considered a member of the moderate wing of the Court. Souter had been on the Court only one year when the *Simon & Schuster* case was heard. In a case decided earlier in the year, *Cohen v. Cowles*, Souter had voted with the minority and in his dissent had said that the First Amendment's guarantee of free speech extended beyond the speaker to members of the public who might want to hear the speech (or read it in published form). "Freedom of the press is ultimately founded on the value of enhancing such [public] discourse for the sake of a citizenry better informed," he wrote, "and thus more prudently self-governed."

ORAL ARGUMENTS BEGIN

An appearance before the U.S. Supreme Court can be the highlight, or the low point, of an attorney's professional life. The justices expect a lawyer to be well prepared, to respond to their questions, to be knowledgeable about relevant cases, and to make his or her arguments within the allotted thirty minutes. A large, round clock hangs above the justices' heads as a reminder of the time limit. For those who need a more emphatic warning, a red light blinks on after thirty minutes have passed, indicating that the time for argument has ended. Chief Justice Rehnquist often stopped a long-winded lawyer in the middle of a sentence when the red light signaled that time was up.

On the morning of Tuesday, October 15, 1991, the court crier intoned the traditional call *Oyez, oyez, oyez* (Hear ye, . . .) as Chief Justice Rehnquist and seven associate justices took their seats behind the massive mahogany bench in the Court chamber. Throughout the proceedings, the justices engaged in a lively exchange of questions and comments that sometimes brought laughter from the audience. As the petitioner, Simon & Schuster presented its arguments first. The publisher's attorney, Ronald S. Rauchberg, strove to convince the justices that because New York's law targeted speech, it violated the First Amendment. The law, he said, applied "to works of expression and only to works of expression."

CRIME PROCEEDS

In answer to a question from Justice O'Connor, the publisher's lawyer acknowledged that New York and many other states had laws that required criminals to forfeit the tools used in crimes and the proceeds of criminal acts. In other words, a drug dealer convicted of transporting drugs in his yacht would lose the vessel as well as any money from drug sales confiscated by police. Under that law, a justice pointed out, New York could have taken action against financier Michael Milken to collect any profits he made from illegal trading. One justice suggested that payments for a book on crime could also be considered proceeds of crime. "But for his commission of the crime, he wouldn't have this knowledge that he's making money on," the justice noted.

But Rauchberg quickly differentiated the proceeds of a crime from the royalties collected for a book written about the crime. In making his case, Rauchberg cited *The Autobiography of Malcolm X*, a book based on writer Alex Haley's interviews with the black leader. The work, which was published not long after Malcolm X's death in 1965, begins with extensive descriptions of the subject's early life in crime and details his transformation into an important leader in the black community's struggle for civil rights.

The royalties Malcolm X earned for the book should not be considered "crime proceeds," Rauchberg argued. "They are instead the earnings of an author in the typical way that authors earn money, through being who they are and through the sweat of their brow."

Under New York's Son of Sam law, however, the royalties would have been considered proceeds of a crime and added to the escrow fund set up by the state. "I

A reader looks at books written by and about Malcolm X. The black activist's autobiography, written by Alex Haley, might have been affected by the Son of Sam law if the statute had been in effect when the book was published.

suggest that that's not correct," the lawyer said. "The crime is a separate act from the authorship of a book. The authorship of a book is an act to be encouraged, not an act to be suppressed."

Justice Kennedy asked if the lawyer's statement would cover "a lurid account" of a rape. Rauchberg countered that even in that case, the Court should not discourage the writing of books. "My position is that the First Amendment encourages the writing of all books, and it is not for this Court to distinguish between which books should be encouraged and which books should not.

"And more to the point, it is not for the State of New York to decide that books on a specified subject, namely crime, by a specified class of authors, namely criminals as defined, are books to be discouraged as opposed to encouraged."

DISTORTING THE DEBATE

Rauchberg said that Son of Sam laws that interfered with the publication of books based on their content led to "distortion in the marketplace of ideas." Even if the First Amendment allowed it, separating the books that should have royalties put in escrow from those that should not would be too difficult a task. He listed four classes of people whose stories might not be told because of the New York law: abortion protesters, animal rights activists, terminally ill patients considering suicide, and battered women who had protected themselves with violence. If the state could take their royalties, these people might not write or share their stories, and "an important part of the public debate on those four issues" would be lost, Rauchberg said. He noted that people on other sides of the issue—victims, prosecutors, police officers—could tell their story and get paid for it without interference. The Son of Sam law, he argued, would prevent the public from getting the complete story because the person charged in the crime (the protester, the activist, the would-be suicide, the battered woman) would not be heard.

Even with the law in place, a justice said, the publisher could still commission books by criminals. True, Rauchberg responded, but he added that few authors could afford to work for free. "If you can't compensate an author," he said, "you will get less authorship." He noted that Henry Hill expected compensation and got it, but only because the publisher did not comply with the law. "Hill wanted a publishing contract, and so in this case, this book, which is . . . being called the best book about crime written in America, could only have been written as a result of making payments to the person whose information was essential to its creation."

During the discussion, Justice Scalia compared the issue of royalties to Italian sculptor Benvenuto Cellini's account of a thief who stole a precious metal and used it to craft a beautiful statue. "Does the statue belong to the person from whom the bronze was stolen?" he asked. He drew laughter when he admitted, "I forget what the answer was." He noted that the parable could be applied to the Henry Hill case. "I think that's the same problem we're talking about here . . . someone who embellishes by his artistry the account of the crime."

Rauchberg, however, contended that Hill and others like him did more than "embellish" the crime. Jean Harris, for example, wrote eloquently about prison conditions—a topic completely separate from her crime—but the New York board seized her royalties because she mentioned her crime in two of the book's fourteen chapters. "The whole book gets treated as though it's crime proceeds," he said.

Hill himself talked about many topics in *Wiseguys* in addition to his own crimes. He described the operation of the mob, the corrupt prison system that allowed certain inmates to conduct illegal activities behind bars, and the activities of crooked politicians and others who aided the crime family.

In other instances, Rauchberg said, criminals profited from their notoriety, which they used to sell books and articles, appear on talk shows, and market a variety of products and services. New York's law did not touch that income as long as the criminal did not mention his or her specific crimes. Instead, it targeted speech-related activities. "And since laws targeted at speech inevitably will deter some of the speech at which they're targeted, it's what condemns the law under the First Amendment," Rauchberg concluded.

LAW TOO BROAD

In addressing another point, Rauchberg said that New York's law targeted far too broad a range of people. In addition to convicted criminals, its provisions applied to those merely accused of crimes as well as to people who admitted in their books that they had committed certain illegal acts for which they were never charged. Henry Hill, the lawyer pointed out, had been granted immunity for his crimes in return for testifying against the mob. In response to questioning from the Court, Rauchberg said that New York's Criminal Victims Board could seize money from authors who had committed certain acts that the board itself determined were crimes even if the authors did not see them as illegal. Hill did not say he had violated specific laws, Rauchberg noted. He merely described his behavior.

Justice O'Connor asked whether it would be acceptable for a state to pass a law that required all the assets of criminals be placed in escrow to pay the victims of their crimes. Rauchberg said such a law would be acceptable because it would not target only assets produced by speech that contained certain content (mention of crimes).

Another justice wanted to know if such a law would not also discourage criminals from writing books. Rauchberg replied that a law that applied to all assets would put all types of jobs on an equal playing field without singling out speech-related activities. The assets of most criminals, he noted, did not come from books and movies anyway. It made no sense to have a law that seized only profits from writing, when most criminals had more money from other assets.

Rauchberg reserved the few remaining minutes allotted to him so that he could offer a final rebuttal to the position of Assistant Attorney General Zwickel, who would speak next for New York's Crime Victims Board.

VICTIMS ABOVE CRIMINALS

Zwickel began by emphasizing that the law was intended to prevent criminals from profiting from their crimes and to help victims of those crimes. He also noted that Hill had been convicted of various crimes in addition to those merely mentioned in the book.

In the lawyer's view, Hill's advance and royalties should indeed be considered proceeds of a crime. "The statute is directed against that asset because that asset is directly attributable to [Hill's] wrongful conduct." The law, Zwickel added, had "a compelling purpose" in seizing Hill's payments because his story flowed from his illegal actions. "When the criminal discusses his crime and is paid money for that discussion, . . . the criminal is then profiting directly from his victimization."

Zwickel took issue with one justice's suggestion that the "underlying premise" of New York's law was to discourage criminals' accounts of their crimes. "The statute is neutral with respect to the speech," he countered. "If the criminal wants to discuss his story and say anything he wants, but doesn't make a dollar on that discussion, this statute does not apply." When passing the law, the legislature focused on "the unfairness, the inequity" of criminals, but not victims, making a profit from the story of the crime, Zwickel said.

Justice O'Connor quizzed him about the financial burden the law imposed on a criminal author. Zwickel agreed with O'Connor that the law focused only on speech "of a particular content" and acknowledged that "some people will choose not to speak because they are not getting the profits." But he contended that the law inflicted only an "incidental" burden on criminals, who could speak their minds without financial profit. The forfeiture of royalties, unlike the tax burden imposed on publishers in the *Arkansas Writers' Project* case, did not affect publishers or other media, Zwickel said. "The record in this case shows that many criminals will speak and will continue to speak with these statutes [in place]. The publishers keep their profit. The publishers are not compelled to edit material out of the book."

Justice O'Connor asked why the state did not extend the law to cover all the assets earned by criminals. "Why just publishing a book?"

Zwickel replied that it was not fair for criminals to profit from the story of a crime while victims directly affected by the crimes related in that story received no compensation. Such an obvious inequity, Zwickel said, would not occur when other products were involved. "When [David] Berkowitz sits down for an interview and talks about why he killed these . . . people, and then is paid $100,000 for that, it seems to me that New York and the other States can say, well, we can't stop his speech. In fact, he has a right to speak. But he does not have a right to profit before his victims [do]."

The lawyer's argument, however, did not satisfy the justices. Justice Scalia noted that the law did not "nicely [cut] out the profits that [Hill] is making because of his recount of the crime." Instead, said Scalia, the law required that Hill forfeit all the payments he received for the entire book. He likened it to St. Augustine's account of stealing an apple in his autobiographical book, *Confessions*, written in the fourth century. "I assume that . . . whatever St. Augustine got for that book,"—the audience greeted this comment with laughter—"the whole amount . . . would be considered proceeds of the apple-stealing?"

Zwickel quickly agreed that would be the case. Justice Scalia, however, could not contain his disdain. "But that's ridiculous," he exclaimed, eliciting more laughs from those in the courtroom.

PRESERVING THE ASSETS

Ignoring the justice's outburst, the lawyer for the members of the Criminal Victims Board soldiered on. He noted that the law encouraged victims to sue for damages from criminals who profited from publishing their story. Because of the law, such profits would be held in escrow until the suit could be resolved in court. Otherwise, Zwickel said, criminals might spend all the assets they collected from books, movies, and other speech-related ventures before the victims could get paid.

This brought on more comparisons from the justices. Chief Justice Rehnquist theorized that Billy the Kid would have forfeited royalties for a book he might have written about the twenty-one men he killed, but not for another hypothetical book on his "travels in the Southwest." The chief justice noted that a victim who had won court-ordered damages ordinarily should be able to collect proceeds from both books.

Zwickel responded that the New York law would not preclude victims from collecting money from books of both types after proving their case in court. What it did, in the words of Justice White, was allow the state to collect the money "in advance" on books that mentioned the author's crimes. The law accomplished three things, Zwickel said. First, it preserved the royalties at the time the money was paid. Second, it allowed victims to collect after the statute of limitations had expired. Except in the most serious cases, like murder, there is a time limit (statute of limitations) on when a state can bring charges against a criminal suspect. After a certain amount of time has passed, the person can no longer be tried for the crime. Under New York's law, however, victims could reclaim damages up to five years after the criminal signed the book or movie contract. That could occur many years after the original crime was committed, well beyond the statute of limitations imposed by the law. Third, the law directed that victims be paid before other creditors.

In the case of books not regulated by the law, victims could still collect damages if a court so decreed—and if the money had not already been spent.

The "critical issue" before the Court, Zwickel maintained, was whether the state had "appropriately balanced the competing interests" and had developed a law narrowly targeted to accomplish its purpose—which he said was "to ensure that people who commit wrongful acts do not profit directly from their victimization."

The justices pointed out that if the state had truly wanted to make sure that no criminals received any proceeds from their crimes, legislators would have passed a bill that included victimless crimes [like prostitution]. "Do you agree that it is fair to say that the object is not to preclude the criminal from directly profiting, the object is simply to preclude him from profiting before the victims get paid?" Justice Souter asked.

Zwickel affirmed that the state's law focused on the "unfairness of the criminal profiting before his victims" but noted that states and the federal government still had "valid interests in stopping criminals from profiting from crime." New York's Son of Sam law, he emphasized, was "more narrowly tailored" to concentrate on victim compensation.

He spent the waning moments of his argument trying to portray New York's law as a statute that met the "strict scrutiny" test and that did not target speech based on content. "I want to emphasize again," he said, "that this statute is not simply limited to one type of book or one type of speech. It is a broad-based statute which applies in any context where a criminal is profiting from the story of his crime." He said once more that the law merely ensured that money would be available to victims who won their suits for damages. "The statute," he concluded, "is targeted precisely to its purpose and its purpose is both a legitimate purpose and a compelling one."

LAST WORDS

In the two minutes remaining of his half-hour presentation, Rauchberg denied that Hill had been convicted of any crimes linked to the state's action in the case. Even if the book had referred to crimes for which Hill had been convicted, the lawyer said, he would still oppose the law on the grounds that it violated the First Amendment. "I say we have to tolerate whatever offense [criminals write about] . . . in order to have the valuable speech that we have when other criminals like Henry David Thoreau, Malcolm X, Martin Luther King, and many others named in our briefs, have written books that make reference to their crimes."

Chief Justice Rehnquist thanked the lawyers and submitted the case to the Court for judgment. This is the point at which the justices participating in a decision begin to discuss behind closed doors the issues addressed in the briefs and in oral arguments. Following custom, when it comes time to vote on a case, the chief justice speaks first and the associate justices make their views known in order of seniority. Then the justices take an initial vote. If the chief justice votes with the majority, he writes the decision for the Court or appoints an associate justice also on the winning side to compose the opinion. When the chief justice is on the losing side, the most-senior associate justice who has voted with the majority assigns the task.

Justices on either side often write separate opinions expressing their views on a case, a dissent when they disagree with the majority and a concurrence when they support the final outcome but have different reasons for doing so. Sometimes, after reading their colleagues' drafts, justices change their vote. If the vote shifts to the other side, then a justice voting with the majority must write a new decision.

Justice Sandra Day O'Connor wrote the unanimous Supreme Court decision in the *Simon & Schuster* case, which struck down New York's Son of Sam law.

THE DECISION AND ITS AFTERMATH

ON DECEMBER 10, 1991, THE U.S. SUPREME COURT struck down New York's Son of Sam law. In a unanimous decision, the Court ruled that the law violated the First Amendment guarantee of freedom of speech. Justice Sandra Day O'Connor wrote the 8-to-0 decision.

Justice O'Connor acknowledged that states had "a compelling interest in ensuring that victims of crime are compensated by those who harm them." She noted, however, the state could adopt other measures to accomplish that goal. Therefore, New York's law placed an unconstitutional burden on criminals' speech.

INFRINGING RIGHTS

The Court had no doubt that the New York law infringed on First Amendment rights. The law, wrote O'Connor, "plainly imposes a financial disincentive only on speech of a particular content." Only assets from books or other speech-related activities that mentioned the author's (or contributor's) crimes came under the law's provisions. Those provisions deprived criminal authors of their royalties unless no victims claimed them within five years.

A statute was presumed to be "inconsistent with the First Amendment," O'Connor said in her opinion, whenever that law imposed a financial burden on speakers based on the content of what they say. In fact, she noted, the notion was "so engrained in our First Amendment" system of law that the Court had not even bothered to explain the "obvious" tenet in a previous ruling. To bolster that conclusion, Justice O'Connor quoted Justice John M. Harlan's 1971 ruling in *Cohen v. California*, which she had also cited in her decision in *Leathers v. Medlock* earlier in the Court's 1991 term. Harlan's ruling read in part:

> The constitutional right of free expression is . . . intended to remove governmental restraints from the arena of public discussion, putting the decision as to what views shall be voiced largely into the hands of each of us . . . in the belief that no other approach would comport with the premise of individual dignity and choice upon which our political system rests.

She rejected the board's claim that because the statute's purpose was not to suppress certain ideas, there was no violation of the First Amendment. The First Amendment bars laws from interfering with speech even when the government has valid concerns and its aim is not to censor speech, O'Connor wrote in her eighteen-page opinion.

The Son of Sam law placed a financial burden on speech, the justice noted, and it did not matter who was identified as the "speaker" in the case—Henry Hill, whose royalties were placed in escrow for five years, or Simon & Schuster, whose ability to publish books about crime was hampered by the law.

COMPELLING STATE INTERESTS

The Court has allowed some state laws to infringe on citizens' rights—but only when a state can show that the law was the only way to meet "compelling" state interests. To justify the law's interference with the right of free speech, the state had to show that its statute was "narrowly drawn" to achieve "a compelling state interest," O'Connor said, quoting from Justice Thurgood Marshall's decision in the *Arkansas Writers' Project* case. In *Simon & Schuster*, the government failed to meet this requirement.

The Court accepted only one of the state's two compelling interests in enacting the law—the importance of compensating victims. While the state also had "an undisputed compelling interest in insuring that criminals do not profit from their crimes," the law did not accomplish that goal, O'Connor said. She noted that the board had given no credible reason why criminals should be deprived of speech-based assets but not assets from other activities or why victims would benefit from one type of asset but not the other. "The distinction drawn by the Son of Sam law [between speech-related assets and assets from other sources such as property or job earnings] has nothing to do with the State's interest in transferring the proceeds of crime from criminals to their victims," the justice stated.

O'Connor also noted that the Court could make a ruling in the case without deciding whether book royalties should or should not be considered profits of crime. The Court was concerned only with the infringement of speech—not how the speech was categorized.

Even the state's compelling interest in compensating victims, however, could not justify infringing on First Amendment rights, O'Connor said, because the law was "significantly overinclusive," and because there were other ways to accomplish the goal. The justice found fault with two sections of New York's law: First, it was too broad in that it included works on any subject in which the author expressed thoughts, feelings, or recollections about a crime. In addition, the statute's definition of "criminal," which included individuals who had never been charged or convicted of illegal acts, covered too many people. "Those two provisions," wrote the justice, "combine to encompass a potentially very large number of works."

She noted that a publishers' group had submitted a list of hundreds of works that could be subject to the law. Among these writings by U.S. prisoners and former prisoners were books by Martin Luther King Jr. and Emma Goldman, a prominent political activist of the early twentieth century. New York's Son of Sam law, Justice O'Connor concluded, was "too overinclusive to satisfy the requirements of the First Amendment:"

Should a prominent figure write his autobiography at the end of his career, and include in an early chapter a brief recollection of having stolen (in New York) a nearly worthless item as a youthful prank, the Board would control his entire income from the book for five years, and would make that income available to all of the author's creditors, despite the fact that the statute of limitations for this minor incident had long since run [out]. That the Son of Sam law can produce such an outcome indicates that the statute is, to say the least, not narrowly tailored to achieve the State's objective of compensating crime victims from the profits of crime.

Emma Goldman (*left*) works on her memoirs with her secretary, Emily Holmes Coleman.

Because the New York law's too-broad provisions made it unconstitutional, O'Connor said, there was no need to rule on whether the law also violated the First Amendment by regulating speech based on its content.

Justice O'Connor noted the critical acclaim the book received and quoted several passages of *Wiseguy*, including a section on the corruption of the prison system, which allowed jailed mobsters to live in style:

> We had the best food smuggled into our dorm from the kitchen. Steaks, veal cutlets, shrimp, red snapper. Whatever the hacks [prison guards] could buy, we ate. It cost me two, three hundred a week. Guys like Paulie [Vario] spent five

hundred to a thousand bucks a week. Scotch cost thirty dollars a pint. The hacks used to bring it inside the walls in their lunch pails. We never ran out of booze, because we had six hacks bringing it in six days a week.

In closing, Justice O'Connor said that other states and the federal government had their own Son of Sam laws, some of which might be "quite different" from the one being considered. The Court, she cautioned, was not determining whether all such laws were unconstitutional, only the statute in New York.

TWO CONCURRENCES

Two justices, Blackmun and Kennedy, filed separate opinions. Both justices supported the final outcome but wanted to add their views on the issue. These concurrences became part of the official Court record but did not have the weight of the majority opinion, which future justices would rely on to make rulings on similar matters.

In a terse, three-sentence opinion, Justice Blackmun said the Court should not have rejected the law solely because it was too broad. The decision should also have dealt with the fact that the law targeted only speech of a certain content. He said that other states had similar laws and deserved better guidance from the Court.

In his concurrence, Justice Kennedy also called on

the Court to focus on the law's restrictions on speech based on content. He argued that the law should have been rejected on that ground alone. Restricting speech on the basis of content, he said, violated the First Amendment under any circumstances. New York's statute, he noted, imposed "severe restrictions" on speech, "using as its sole criterion the content of what is written." Criminals' speech about their crimes, he contended, had "the full protection of the First Amendment." That, he concluded, was "itself a full and sufficient reason for holding the statute unconstitutional."

Kennedy held further that the Court was "ill advised" to explore further arguments based on a state's compelling interests and whether the law was narrow enough to meet the Court's requirements. "All that is at issue [in this case] is a content-based restriction," the justice wrote. To conduct further analysis, he said, "might be read as a concession that States may censor speech whenever they believe there is a compelling justification for doing so. Our precedents and traditions allow no such inference." In support of his argument, Kennedy quoted from the Court's ruling in the 1972 case, *Police Department of Chicago v. Mosely*: "Regulations which permit the Government to discriminate on the basis of the content of the message cannot be tolerated under the First Amendment."

Even if New York State had presented compelling

reasons that met the Court's requirements, Kennedy said, the law still should have been rejected. The speech regulated by the law was not obscene, not defamatory, not likely to incite unlawful acts or cause imminent harm that the state could prevent. Those were the traditional conditions under which government could regulate the content of speech under the Constitution, the justice said. Since the speech affected by New York's law did not fall into any of those categories, "no further inquiry [was] necessary to reject the State's argument."

The justice acknowledged that in recent years the Court had allowed the regulation of other types of speech, such as child pornography, but he said that in *Simon & Schuster*, the Court should have relied on historic decisions that upheld free-speech protections. Otherwise, he warned, the Court risked weakening "central protections of the First Amendment." Kennedy concluded that the Court should have ruled "that the New York statute amounts to raw censorship based on content, censorship forbidden by the text of the First Amendment and well-settled principles protecting speech and the press."

PROTECTING RIGHTS

First Amendment proponents hailed the Court's decision. "On the core issues of the First Amendment, this court is very solid," said New York attorney Charles S. Sims, one of the lawyers on Simon & Schuster's team.

Attorney Steven Shapiro, who had helped prepare the ACLU brief supporting the publisher's position, called the ruling "far-reaching." He added, "The fact that the decision was unanimous I think sends a very strong message that this court will not tolerate laws that penalize speech because of what is being said."

Members of the media commended the Court for the opinion. In its editorial on the ruling, the *New York Times* wrote: "Laws like New York's deserve to fall if they invite government to pick and choose among ideas and the people who express them." The editorial said states could target criminals' assets and turn them over to victims without focusing exclusively on speech. The Court, in its ruling, "struck a unanimous blow for press freedom," the *Las Vegas Review-Journal* wrote in its editorial pages. New York's Son of Sam law, the editor wrote, had been enacted "out of some misguided sense of outrage" and "set a dangerous and unwieldy precedent that would surely have come back to haunt its proponents."

Richard E. Snyder, chair of Simon & Schuster, savored the victory, saying he was "gratified" by the ruling. The Court's decision, he said, was "a major victory for freedom of speech and for writers, publishers and the reading public." Another publisher told the *New York Times* that several books had not seen publication because of the Son of Sam law, but the ruling would change that: "This ruling says that committing a crime does not deprive a person of his most fundamental constitutional right to speak his mind and tell his story." Snyder reiterated the company's position that victims could still receive compensation from criminals' assets, including royalties from books about their crimes. "We said from the outset that this case was not about compensating victims of crimes. It was about protecting the right to tell all sides of a story."

Nicholas Pileggi, who wrote the book central to the case, declared his support for a revised law that would set aside money for victims. "I have no problem with a law compensating victims of crimes," he said. "But the old law put a body slam on the First Amendment." Noting that books on crime served useful purposes, Pileggi pointed out that the FBI used *Wiseguy* as an instruction manual on how the mob operated.

Not everyone involved in publishing applauded the ruling. Stephen Michaud, author of *Murderers Among Us: Unsolved Homicides, Mysterious Deaths, and Killers at Large*, a true-crime book, denounced the Court's decision. He speculated that the lure of fame and lucrative book and film contracts might even encourage criminals to commit sensational crimes. "If you look at it from a criminal's point of view, the Supreme Court is saying you can get paid for killing," he said. "[Mass killers are] right now saying, 'Here's the answer to my problems. Not only will I get famous, but rich, too.'"

BIDDING WARS

The ruling received mixed reviews from other groups. Many state legislators and victims' rights advocates denounced the decision. The New York state senator who had sponsored the law, Emanuel Gold, said the decision "disgusted" him. He vowed to introduce new legislation that would withstand the Court's scrutiny. Mario M. Cuomo, governor of New York, announced that his office would research writing a new law that would not violate the Constitution. In addition to New York's law, officials expected the decision to invalidate legislation in most of the other forty-one states with Son of Sam laws.

Jim Van Messel, a producer of the television show *Entertainment Tonight*, believed the overturning of the Son of Sam law would spur a bidding war for crime stories: "This is just going to encourage another form of ambulance-chasing. . . . Agents and authors can hear about a crime and go after the person who did it and say: 'Let me represent you and I'll make you a star.' It's always been big business, selling stories to the media, and this is just going to make it bigger."

The producer of *A Current Affair*, John Terenzio, agreed, saying, "There is no doubt that for the infamous kind of crimes, there will be a lot of activity to get those rights. The broadcast media and publishers and movie studios will have a new domain, and they'll move into it, some more aggressively than others."

Robin Douglas places a flower next to a photograph of her son, Lamar Whitehead, during Crime Victims' Rights Week. Lamar was killed in a carjacking in 2005.

Victims' rights advocates and others feared that the decision would allow criminals to pocket huge amounts of cash while their victims would never be compensated. "The more notorious the crime, clearly the more funds will be offered," said Paul Hudson, who once served as counsel to the New York State Crime Victims Board. "Now that the lid is off, criminals will be hiring agents to create bidding wars to get them top dollar. The sky would be the limit, and publishers and movie producers could slip vast amounts of money secretly to criminals without their victims ever knowing."

Barbara Leak, the chair of the New York Crime Victims Board, called it "a blow to victims' rights." She added: "We need to be able to say you can't get profits from being a wrongdoer." Richard Samp, a spokesman for the Washington Legal Foundation (WLF), expressed similar views. "Crime victims are left feeling as though the people who victimize them can gain doubly from their crime," he said. The WLF, a conservative nonprofit public policy organization, devotes much of its effort to advocating for crime victims.

Media specialists and attorneys on both sides, however, offered another view. They speculated that victims could benefit from the decision because it would boost criminals' assets and enable crime victims to collect larger damages. Current law allowed victims of crimes to sue criminals in civil court for damages related to their crimes. Gerald Boyle, the lawyer representing serial killer Jeffrey Dahmer, said his client had already been approached by writers and movie studios interested in negotiating a deal. Ironically, the ruling allowing criminals to sell their stories might accomplish the same results as a crime victims board, Boyle said. "My client and his family, especially his father, are most interested in finding a mechanism to compensate the victims' families."

Ricci Adan, the widow of the man stabbed to death by Jack Henry Abbott, stood to gain all of the royalties due from the killer's book *In the Belly of the Beast* and other works; the total amount included about $15,000 held in escrow by the New York Crime Victims Board. In 1990 a Massachusetts court awarded Mrs. Adan damages of $7.5 million in a wrongful death civil suit. Daniel P. Leonard, the Adan family lawyer, said the court had ordered an attachment on any assets Abbott acquired. "We didn't really need the 'Son of Sam' rule," Leonard said. With the court award, he said, "my clients basically own Jack Abbott. He could spend the rest of his life typing away, but he'd have to earn $12 million before he sees a penny of it." He predicted that the market for crime stories would grow quickly with the Court's decision clearing the way. "Once that happens, criminals will believe they'll have a freer hand to get contracts—and then there'll be more money for victims to go after."

PAYDAY FOR HILL AND OTHERS

After the decision was announced, reporters heard from Henry Hill, still in hiding at the time. "It was a nice Christmas present," Hill told one reporter. "Okay, fine, I led a nefarious life, but I changed—I put my life and my family at risk. Eleven years looking over my shoulder, helping out the government. I felt in all honesty I should be paid for my work." He was due to receive about $200,000 for his work on the book *Wiseguy* and the movie *GoodFellas*, including royalties held by the Crime Victims Board. Additional royalties later increased his payoff on the film to more than half a million dollars.

Other criminals also expected payoffs after the Court's ruling. R. Foster Winans had forfeited $20,000 to the New York Crime Victims Board after his conviction for fraud in 1985. The proceeds came from his book *Trading Secrets*,

Henry Hill collected a big payoff in royalties after the Supreme Court decision.

in which Winans, a former financial reporter for the *Wall Street Journal*, detailed his involvement in an insider trading scheme. Another white-collar criminal, Dennis Levine, had royalties in escrow from his book *Inside Out*, his firsthand account of insider trading and Wall Street scandal.

The victims board also held $8,626 from proceeds earned by Mark David Chapman, John Lennon's assassin, for his contributions to an article on the murder published in 1987 by *People* magazine.

The *Simon & Schuster* ruling also meant that the board would have to turn over about $100,000 to Jean Harris for royalties on her book *Stranger in Two Worlds*. She pledged the money to a foundation she had founded to benefit the children of her fellow prison inmates.

CHAPTER SIX

FREE SPEECH VS. PROFITS FROM CRIME

AS SOON AS THE COURT DELIVERED ITS OPINION, New York lawmakers and other interested parties began exploring ways to rewrite the law to comply with the Constitution. In 1992 the state legislature passed a new version of the law. It applied only to people convicted of crimes under New York's laws.

The new law came under scrutiny in the spring of 1997 when the New York Crime Victims Board and the state attorney general sued publisher HarperCollins and author Peter Maas to recover payments from the publication of *Underboss*, the best-selling story of Salvatore "Sammy the Bull" Gravano and his life in organized crime. Gravano's testimony helped bring down mobster John Gotti Sr., head of the Gambino crime family. Gravano revealed that he had split an $850,000 advance with Maas for his contribution to the work. The Mafia informer also said he expected to earn additional royalties from a planned film version of the book. Gravano admitted to killing nineteen people, but under a plea deal with prosecutors he was convicted of racketeering under the federal RICO (Racketeer Influenced and Corrupt Organizations) act. He ultimately served five years in prison on that charge after testifying against Gotti.

Lawyers for the defendants challenged the constitutionality of the 1992 law, which they said had the same flaws as the previous one, struck down by the Supreme Court in 1991. Additionally, the lawyers argued, the law did not apply to Gravano because he had been convicted for violating federal laws, not the laws of New York. Maas's attorney called the suits "offensive in every sense of the word legally" and said New York's law was a modern-day form of "book burning." Such laws, he said, had "a chilling impact on the storytellers of the world."

In a unanimous decision, the New York Court of Appeals ruled against the Crime Victims Board. The decision, issued March 7, 2000, determined that the New York law did not apply in the case because Gravano had been convicted of a federal, not a state, crime (racketeering). In addition, the court ruled that the Crime Victims Board did not have authority to bring legal action against Gravano because no victim of his crime had filed a petition with the board.

Attorney Slade R. Metcalf, who represented Harper-Collins in the suit, called the ruling a landmark decision, which "makes clear that authors and publishers can publish accounts of criminal activity without fear of interference from the Crime Victims Board."

Son of Sam laws in two other states were considered in the courts in 2002. California's Supreme Court struck down that state's statute, which it said "violates constitutional protections of speech" when it leads to the confiscation of convicted criminals' payments for "expressive materials that include the story of the crime." The case involved the 1963 kidnapping of Frank Sinatra Jr., the son of the noted singer. Three men, Barry Keenan, Joseph Amsler, and John Irwin, were later convicted of felonies in connection with the crime. Years after their release from prison, the kidnappers arranged to have writer Peter Gilstrap interview them for a tabloid story on the kidnapping. The article, printed in *New Times Los Angeles* in January 1998, became the basis of a movie produced by Columbia Pictures. The younger Sinatra filed a complaint in superior court to prevent the kidnappers, *New Times*, and Columbia Pictures from collecting profits on the story. Under the Son of Sam law, Sinatra claimed, the proceeds should go to a trust and be turned over to him as the victim of the crime.

Like New York's law, California's statute required that proceeds earned by criminals from projects that

Frank Sinatra Jr. talks to reporters after his kidnappers freed him in 1963.

included an account of their crimes be put into a trust for victims of the crimes. The law included a long list of pertinent projects: books, films, magazine and newspaper articles, video and sound recordings, radio and television appearances, and live presentations. An exception was made for instances in which the crime was mentioned in a footnote or bibliography. California first enacted its law in 1983 and amended it several times after the U.S. Supreme Court delivered its ruling in the *Simon & Schuster* case. Unlike the invalidated New York law,

California's statute applied only to felony convictions. In 1994 the state legislature expanded the law to include profits from memorabilia and other items valued for their "felony-related notoriety." Lawmakers also barred "profiteers" from collecting the proceeds from the sale of such goods.

The lower court granted a temporary injunction to block the payments to the kidnappers. On appeal, the court upheld Sinatra's position. The California Supreme Court, however, overruled the lower courts. In its decision, the court determined that the law, like that of New York, was too broad, even though it was limited to convicted felons and exempted mentions of crimes in footnotes. If a criminal included the story of his or her crime in a speech, a book, or other work, the law allowed the state to confiscate earnings for the entire production, which the court ruled was a violation of free speech. As written, the law could discourage "a wide range of expressive works" that fell under the First Amendment's protection. The court presented a long list of examples in which a criminal had to mention past crimes in order to produce a valid and valuable work: a discussion of personal redemption, a warning to others of crime's consequences, an evaluation of the criminal justice system, an exposé of corruption, a description of prison conditions, or an "inside look at the criminal underworld," as Henry Hill had provided.

A proposed Massachusetts law met a similar fate at the hands of that state's Supreme Judicial Court. In an unusual move that eased the concerns of authors and publishers, the court issued an advisory opinion to the state senate, declaring that the Son of Sam bill under consideration would violate the First Amendment and the state's constitutional guarantees of free speech. Based on the court's advice, the Massachusetts legislature did not pass the bill.

In 2004 the Nevada Supreme Court struck down that state's Son of Sam law for the same reasons cited in *Simon & Schuster v. Members of the New York Crime Victims Board*: the statute was too broad. The case involved Jimmy Lerner, whose prison memoir, *You Got Nothing Coming: Notes From a Prison Fish*, came out in 2001. A gripping account of life behind bars, the book ended with a description of Lerner's crime: the manslaughter strangling of a friend. The victim's sister sued in 2002 to collect proceeds from the book under Arizona's Son of Sam law. The court dismissed the suit based on First Amendment concerns.

"It is very clear that these laws chill free speech," Lerner's attorney, Scott Freeman, said. "They not only violate the First Amendment rights of people like Mr. Lerner who engage in expressive work, but people also have a constitutional right to read books like his and receive information."

ANOTHER WAY TO COLLECT

David Berkowitz, the New York killer whose crimes spurred the passage of the Son of Sam law, gained a following among fundamentalist Christians after the publication of a book titled *Son of Hope: The Prison Journals of David Berkowitz*. Volume 1 of the journals details Berkowitz's conversion to Christianity and his work with fellow inmates. His newfound friends in the fundamentalist movement set up a website to promote the book, for which Berkowitz says he receives no money.

David Berkowitz speaks to an interviewer in 2009. He says he gets no royalties from a book he wrote in prison.

Other crime figures, however, continue to profit from exposés of their lives or are working on book and film projects. John Gotti Jr., who served nine years for mob-related crimes, announced in 2010 that he plans to produce a feature film on his life with his late father, John Gotti Sr., onetime head of the Gambino crime family. In 2011 Karen Gravano, daughter of Sammy the Bull, stood to earn more than a million dollars from her appearance on the reality show *Mob Wives* and a book deal with St. Martin's Press said to reveal her experiences as a child of the mob. She pleaded guilty in 2001 to charges related to a drug operation run by her father, and she and her mother were sentenced to probation.

Whenever a high-profile criminal signs a book or movie deal, outraged citizens push legislators to pass new Son of Sam laws. According to the Freedom Forum, an organization dedicated to protecting constitutional rights, only ten states did not have Son of Sam laws in force at the beginning of the twenty-first century. Three, New Hampshire, North Carolina, and Vermont, had never enacted Son of Sam laws. Seven others—Illinois, Louisiana, Massachusetts, Missouri, Nevada, South Carolina, and Texas—had repealed such laws and never replaced them. Most states had revised their Son of Sam laws after the Supreme Court ruling in *Simon & Schuster*. Many of the laws currently on the books, however, have not addressed the constitutional concerns expressed in the decision and remain largely untested in the courts. Since its decision in the *Simon & Schuster* case, the U.S. Supreme Court has not ruled on any other Son of Sam law.

New York's latest version of the repeatedly revised law applies to criminals convicted of a felony committed in New York or perpetrated against a New York resident. Under the law, anyone who pays convicted felons $10,000 or more must notify the criminals' victims. The victims then have up to three years to sue the wrongdoers to collect for damages. The money can come from almost any source, including gifts and legitimate income. The new law does not specifically mention movies, books, or other speech-related products. The statute has not yet faced Supreme Court scrutiny.

After lower courts knocked down revised Son of Sam laws in several states, officials began to seek other ways to lay claim to criminals' book and film royalties. Claims against the assets of Salvatore Gravano were renewed in Arizona in 2000 after officials there arrested the mobster (then living under the federal witness protection program) on drug distribution charges. Officials then sued Gravano in civil court to collect the assets, including those from his book and a movie based on his story, under a state antiracketeering statute. Arizona law allowed the state to seize "proceeds traceable" to racketeering.

Gravano took the case to the Arizona appeals court, but this time the court ruled against him. In its 2002 decision, the Arizona Superior Court ruled that Arizona's forfeiture law, unlike Son of Sam statutes, did not target only speech-related proceeds and was "content neutral." The court found that "the *Underboss* royalties owed to Gravano may be subject to forfeiture regardless of the message conveyed in the book" if there was "a causal connection" between racketeering and the assets. In his majority opinion, Justice Mark Sanata noted that royalties could not be seized if there was "just a mention of [racketeering] in an expressive work."

Even though the crimes discussed in Gravano's book had been committed in New York, the state claimed that the mobster had used the royalties to finance his illegal drug ring, and thus the proceeds were tied to racketeering conducted in Arizona. The court agreed that Gravano would not have obtained the royalties "but for" his involvement in racketeering. "Without question," Justice Sanata wrote, "it was Gravano's notoriety from that conduct that made his story marketable and of commercial value."

The Arizona Supreme Court and the U.S. Supreme Court rejected Gravano's plea to review the decision. As a result, the state seized $420,000 in royalties from *Underboss*. The money was later divided equally among the eight families of Gravano's victims who had sought compensation from the mobster in court.

Attorney Freeman speculated that other states concerned about the constitutionality of their Son of Sam laws might adopt Arizona's approach. "I think what most states will do is what Arizona did. . . . Arizona cleverly went through the state RICO [Racketeer Influenced and Corrupt Organizations] law. I think more prosecutors will find creative ways to get around the constitutional problems imposed by the Son of Sam decisions." Julie Hilden, a commentator on First Amendment issues, says that such laws "might best be thought of as Son of Sam laws in disguise." RICO laws were originally aimed at organized crime, but officials now use them in prosecutions involving illegal business practices such as extortion and bribery, and obstructing an official investigation.

Another way to avoid the constitutional problems posed by Son of Sam laws is for crime victims to sue criminals for damages in civil court, just as Ricci Adan sued the man who killed her husband. Such suits do not target the products of speech specifically, instead going after all assets a criminal might have. Some states have taken steps to aid victims in civil court suits. The state of California, for example, passed a law in 2002 that extends the statute of limitations so that victims can sue criminals long after a crime was committed—up to ten years after a convict completes parole.

"MURDERABILIA" FOR SALE

Today the Internet has made it much easier for criminals to market their notoriety. Crime-related memorabilia, known as "murderabilia," have attracted many buyers. The items encompass everything from a mass murderer's toenail clippings to guns once owned by criminals. Through an Internet site, Alfred J. Gaynor, convicted of raping and killing four Massachusetts women in 1997 and 1998, has offered for sale bags of his hair, as well as drawings. A go-between in Montreal handles the sales and deposits a portion of the profits in Gaynor's prison account. The Commonwealth of Massachusetts does not have a statute outlawing the sale of crime-related objects by criminals. The mother of one of Gaynor's victims calls his sales "disgusting" and says the serial killer "shouldn't profit from murder." Andy Kahan, a crime victims' advocate in Houston, identifies Gaynor as a "big wheeler dealer" in the murderabilia marketplace. "From a victim's point of view, it's the most nauseating and disgusting feeling in the world" to know that these items are for sale and that there are people eager to buy them, he says.

Public disgust over such sales has led to efforts to bar criminals from profiting from the notoriety brought by their crimes. To do that, however, is no easy task. To attempt to control the sales of crime-related goods on the Internet, experts say, would be "a Herculean task." In 2001 complaints from an appalled public prompted the online auction site eBay to ban the sale of certain items in the murderabilia category. Banned items include human body parts, personal belongings of anyone convicted of a violent crime, and letters and artwork of serial killers or violent felons, among other things. (Because Henry Hill was not convicted of a violent crime, he escapes the eBay ban.) The site allows historical items (more than one hundred years old) and books, documentaries, and movies on violent crimes but bans "any work, such as a book," from which violent felons might profit. Yahoo! has similar policies. Both sites rely on users, however, to report inappropriate items. And anyone, including violent felons, can create a website to sell such memorabilia.

In 2011 only eight states had statutes barring the sale of crime-related items for profit. California law prohibits anyone from profiting from selling memorabilia and other items whose value has been increased by "the notoriety gained from the commission of [a] felony for which the felon was convicted." The law specifically exempts members of the media reporting on a felon's story and materials "where the seller is exercising his or her First Amendment rights."

Texas amended its Son of Sam law in 2003 to require anyone convicted or accused of a crime to turn over proceeds related to the crime, including those from "an Internet website." As in California, Texas law bars sellers from profiting from a criminal's notoriety. New Jersey, Utah, Florida, Alaska, Michigan, and Montana have varying laws that put restrictions on sales of murderabilia. New Jersey, for example, requires murderabilia merchants to put profits from such sales into a state-run escrow fund for victims or pay a $1,000 fine. In 2011 Massachusetts lawmakers were considering a bill to prevent inmates from profiting from "their personal belongings." Several similar bills failed to pass in previous sessions. Many states do not allow prisoners access

SELLING PASTA SAUCE & AUTOGRAPHED ICE PICKS

Henry Hill made several public appearances in 2010 to help celebrate the twentieth anniversary of *GoodFellas*, the acclaimed film based on his account of mob life.

The former mobster has become a celebrity of sorts, using his name to sell everything from watercolors (featuring palm trees or cityscapes and a handgun or two) to pasta sauce (made from a family recipe) to an autographed ice pick on his website and on eBay. A California resident, Hill has appeared several times on the Howard Stern radio show and travels throughout the country showing off his artwork and signing autographs. He has written a cookbook with authentic Italian recipes and *A Goodfella's Guide to New York*. In addition, he is working on a movie based on his involvement in the 1970s point-shaving scheme at Boston College that earned his former associate Jimmy Burke a lengthy prison sentence. In 2007 *Gangsters and Goodfellas: The Mob, Witness Protection, and Life on the Run*, Hill's follow-up to *Wiseguy*, was published. Written with Gus Russo, the book details Hill's life after his decision to testify against the mob. In addition, Hill's two children, Gregg and Gina Hill, wrote their own memoir of their life in hiding, titled *On the Run*.

Nervous but no longer undercover, Hill says that all his old enemies are dead or in jail. "There are some days I can't believe I am still alive," he told reporters gathered at one event. "The gangsters from my past are dead. One or two are still alive but they're serving a 100-year stretch somewhere. I'm the sole survivor, the last man standing." Nevertheless, he remains wary. He received so many nasty e-mails on his website that he created a page devoted to the threat

Henry Hill cuts a pizza into slices in the kitchen of the Nebraska restaurant where he worked as a cook in 2005. Hill has profited from the sale of many items offered over the Internet, including pasta sauce made from an old family recipe.

---

of the week. "I stopped looking over my shoulder maybe 10, 15 years ago," he told a reporter in 2011. "But of course, I worry. I'm still cautious." He told another reporter, "There's always that chance that some young buck wants to make a name for themselves."

When asked what his victims might think about his profiting from his crimes, Hill replied, "I don't give a heck what those people think, I'm doing the right thing now." He noted that many of his victims, but not all, were gangsters themselves and deserved the treatment he gave them.

Notorious gangster John Dillinger's getaway car on display at the National Museum of Crime & Punishment in Washington, D.C.

to computers or the Internet, which makes it more difficult for them to sell items online.

While Internet offerings have recently spurred calls to ban the sale of crime-related memorabilia, such objects have long attracted the public's attention. Entire museums have been established around the topic of crime. In Washington, D.C., the National Museum of Crime & Punishment has on display a number of objects related to crime, including bank robber John Dillinger's getaway car and serial killer Ted Bundy's Volkswagen. The nonprofit organization uses such exhibits to teach lessons in fighting crime and ways to avoid becoming a victim. The Crime Museum (also known as the Black Museum), used by London's Scotland Yard to train recruits, houses a variety of gruesome artifacts from the city's most noted crimes, including the blood-stained underwear of Jack the Ripper's victims and pieces of a bathroom where serial killer Dennis Nilsen dismembered the bodies of young men.

Opposition to laws aimed at crime-related memorabilia comes from several sources. Some say the bans on memorabilia sales would pose a threat to preservation efforts by legitimate historians. Others question whether states can enforce such laws. They note that it is almost impossible to shut off all Internet sales of such items or to determine the identity of sellers, the authenticity of the objects, or whether the criminal tied to an object profits from its sale.

Free-speech proponents and others object to efforts to ban the sale of all objects sold by convicted criminals, including art and other "expressive" work. In 2005 protests erupted when Massachusetts allowed prisoners to display and sell art through an online auction and art show sponsored by the Fortune Society, a nonprofit agency formed to aid prisoners and former prisoners. The controversy revolved around artwork submitted by serial killer Gaynor. Helen Strickland, whose daughter was one of Gaynor's victims, told reporters that the exhibit of his crayon drawing of Christ was "just bringing up wounds on top of wounds and it's like [Gaynor is] some kind of celebrity." A similar uproar in New York in 2002 led that state's corrections commissioner to ban the sale of prisoner art. For thirty-five years before that, prisoners' art had been exhibited once a year and sold, with the profits divided between the artists and the New York Crime Victims Board.

Prisoner advocates argue that encouraging creativity can help rehabilitate even hardened criminals. "For some, you can't punish prisoners enough," says the Reverend William R. Toller, a former prison human services official. But art classes, he believes, help prisoners lead better lives when their sentence is over: "Ninety-nine percent of the guys return to their communities. If we don't give them a sense of hope, then we will pay for that when they are released."

Anthony Papa, who spent twelve years in prison on a drug charge, says his life is proof of the rehabilitative value of art: "The discovery of art allowed me to maintain my humanity," Papa said. "Creating and selling art instills a sense of self-esteem, which is a very important element in re-entering society. Instead of attacking programs like this, we should be expanding them." Papa's self-portrait, exhibited at New York's Whitney Museum of American Art, attracted the attention of New York governor George Pataki, who granted Papa clemency in 1996. That made Papa immediately eligible for parole. Pataki noted that Papa had been a model inmate who had tried to turn his life around while in prison.

THE LAW CANNOT STAND

Ronald Rauchberg, the attorney who represented Simon & Schuster in its landmark First Amendment case, considers the ruling important for two reasons. First, he says, it recognized, "more clearly than in any case before or since," that as a practical matter the First Amendment must protect both speech itself and the payments made for such speech. Quoting Samuel Johnson's famous quip, "No-one but a blockhead ever wrote, except for money," Rauchberg notes, "The court saw the wisdom in [the sentiment expressed by the brilliant eighteenth-century English author] and recognized that limiting the ability to pay for, or to be paid for, certain speech was equivalent to limiting that speech."

Second, the lawyer points out that the Supreme Court made it clear that any time a state infringes on the fundamental rights of its citizens, that action must be justified by extremely compelling public interests: "The case is important as a reminder of how closely and critically the Court will scrutinize such justifications when they are offered," Rauchberg said.

Since delivering the decision in *Simon & Schuster v. Members of the New York Crime Victims Board*, the U.S. Supreme Court, in a number of cases and often by a wide majority, has reaffirmed the free-speech rights of people collecting signatures on petitions, government workers, protesters, politicians, and others. Anthony Kennedy has continued his defense of First Amendment rights in even stronger terms than his fellow justices. In a concurring opinion written in a 2002 case, *Republican Party of Minnesota v. White*, Kennedy again expressed his view that restrictions on speech based on content should automatically be barred. An exception is possible, he says, only when the speech falls within the exceptions traditionally accepted by the Court.

First Amendment lawyer Martin Garbus echoes Kennedy's views: "However much we are revolted by convicted defendants making millions of dollars by writing books, the greater good—namely what we can learn from these books—compels us to encourage, not discourage, them. Where a law is directed to speech alone, if it is not obscene, defamatory, or inflammatory, then the law cannot stand."

THE FIRST AMENDMENT

GUARDIAN OF FUNDAMENTAL RIGHTS

After the American Revolution, citizens set out to create a government for their new nation that would not duplicate Britain's abuses of power that led to war. The Constitution they adopted established a blueprint for the government's operations, while the Bill of Rights protected individual rights from interference by a powerful federal government.

Number one on the Bill of Rights, the First Amendment, guarantees individual Americans some of their most precious rights:

- Freedom to practice their own religious beliefs and a ban on a state religion that would receive preferential treatment over other faiths.
- Freedom to speak without fear of punishment by the government for expressing their views.
- Freedom for the press to publish without interference from the government.
- Freedom to meet in a peaceful manner and associate with whomever they choose.
- Freedom to protest against government actions and to join together to demand change.

In drafting the First Amendment, the founders recognized several principles of American democracy:

- People have a right to freedom (although black Americans were not granted this right until the Thirteenth Amendment abolished slavery).

- Democracy relies on the free expression of its citizenry. To make informed choices about government and their leaders, citizens must have access to a free flow of information. A free "marketplace of ideas" provides citizens with a variety of views and facts on which to evaluate candidates for public office and to assess their performance. Such freedom cannot exist if the government controls the information Americans are allowed to receive.

- The government (and Congress's laws) must not interfere with Americans' basic rights. However, the courts have allowed government to regulate fundamental rights, including freedom of speech, under certain circumstances.

- When rights conflict with each other, the courts must balance them to determine which one has priority. For example, extensive media coverage (freedom of the press) may have an impact on a person's right to a fair trial.

- The First Amendment applies to everyone. Americans are entitled to express their opinions or follow their religion even when other people find such views or religious practices to be offensive.

Since its ratification on December 15, 1791, the First Amendment has stood between Americans and attempts by overzealous moralists, self-promoting politicians, and overreaching officials to stifle dissent, muffle the media, intimidate members of unpopular groups, quell protests, and impose religious views on people whose beliefs are at odds with the majority. The First Amendment has been at the heart of dozens of U.S. Supreme Court cases involving religion or individual beliefs, protest, free speech, and freedom of the press.

The First Amendment often lies at the center of bitter disputes. Despite its lead position in the Bill of Rights, the First Amendment— or at least its interpretation by the courts—has frequently given rise to howls of protest. Does the guarantee of free speech apply to protesters who express their views by burning the flag? Does freedom of the press extend to pornographic magazines and films? Does freedom of religion mean that children cannot sing Christmas carols in public schools? The answers to those questions are not always clear, and court decisions in cases that arise from them are often controversial and unpopular.

Yet that is how a democracy operates. Disputes rage, courts issue rulings, and people use their First Amendment right to free speech to applaud or denigrate the results. It's a free country—in large part because of the protections that the First Amendment provides.

NOTES

INTRODUCTION

p. 8, "Reportedly, a member . . .": Meg Cox, "'Sam' Ruling Likely to Spark Media Scramble," *Wall Street Journal*, December 11, 1991, B1.

p. 9, "It is abhorrent . . .": Senator Emanuel R. Gold, Memorandum, New York State Legislative Annual, 1977, 267. Cited in *Simon & Schuster, Inc. v. Members of New York State Crime Victims Board*, 502 U.S. 105 (1991).

p. 9, "During consideration of,": *Simon & Schuster, Inc. v. Fischetti et al.*, 916 F.2d 777, 59 USLW 2234, 18 Media L. Rep. 1187 (US Ct. of Appeals, 2nd Circuit, 1990).

p. 10, "Berkowitz voluntarily . . .": Editorial, "U.S. Supreme Court Rejects 'Son of Sam' Law on Profits," *San Antonio Express-News*, December 11, 1991, 15A.

CHAPTER ONE

p. 14, "Hill denied . . .": Heather Alexander, "Mafia King on the Straight and Narrow," E24 show, *BBC News*, March 29, 2008, http://news.bbc.co.uk/2/hi/7319520.stm

p. 17, "The Feds . . .": Pete Samson, "OldFella," *The Sun* [London], August 5, 2010, 22.

p. 16, Entire sidebar: N.Y. Exec. Law Sec. 632-a(1); see 1977 N.Y. Laws 823; 1978 N.Y. Laws 417; 1986 N.Y. Laws 74.

p. 17, "The mob ...": Nick Carroll, "Saga of Henry Hill: a Gangster's Old Habits Die Hard, *The Berlin Citizen*, January 12, 2011, http://berlin.ctcitizens.com/story/saga-henry-hill-gangsters-old-habits-die-hard

p. 18, "The author said Hill ...": Vincent Canby, "A Cold-Eyed Look at the Mob's Inner Workings, *New York Times*, September 19, 1990, www.nytimes.com/1990/09/19/movies/review-film-a-cold-eyed-look-at-the-mob-s-inner-workings.html?src=pm

pp. 18–19, "Hearing Hill describe ...": Susan Linfield, "'Goodfellas' Looks at the Banality of Mob Life," *New York Times*, September 16, 1990, www.nytimes.com/1990/09/16/movies/film-goodfellas-looks-at-the-banality-of-mob-life.html?scp=19&sq=Nicholas%20Pileggi&st=cse

p. 19, "We spent more ...": *Simon & Schuster, Inc. v. Members of New York State Crime Victims Board*, 502 U.S. 105 (1991), App. 27.

p. 19, "During his narrative ...": *Simon & Schuster, Inc. v. Members of New York State Crime Victims Board*.

p. 20, "*Times* book reviewer ...": Christopher Lehmann-Haupt, "Books of the Times: Wiseguy: Life in a Mafia Family," *New York Times*, January 16, 1986, www.nytimes.com/1986/01/16/books/books-of-the-times634886.html?scp=2&sq=Nicholas+Pileggi&st=nyt

p. 20, "Columnist Jimmy Breslin ...": *Simon & Schuster, Inc. v. Members of New York State Crime Victims Board*.

p. 20, "the *Washington Post* . . .": *Simon & Schuster, Inc. v. Members of New York State Crime Victims Board.*

p. 21, "It's time . . .": Linfield, "'Goodfellas' Looks at the Banality of Mob Life."

p. 21, "No finer . . .": Roger Ebert, "GoodFellas," *Chicago Sun Times*, September 2, 1990, http://rogerebert.sun times.com/apps/pbcs.dll/article?AID=/19900902/ REVIEWS/9020301/1023

p. 21, "Hill said in 2010 . . .": Nick Allen, "Goodfella Henry Hill still living in hiding 20 years after film release," *The Telegraph*, July 23, 2010. www. telegraph.co.uk/news/worldnews/northamerica/ usa/7906245/Goodfella-Henry-Hill-still-living-in-hiding-20-years-after-film-release.html

p. 23, "The essay . . .": Wendy McElroy, "Henry Thoreau and 'Civil Disobedience,'" *Thoreau Reader*, Future of Freedom Foundation, 2005, http://thoreau.eserver. org/wendy.html

p. 25, "Using the money . . .": *Simon & Schuster, Inc. v. Members of the N.Y. State Crime Victims Bd.*, 724 F. Supp. 170, 177 (S.D.N.Y. 1989).

p. 25, "The law did not . . .": *Simon & Schuster, Inc. v. Fischetti et al.*

CHAPTER TWO

p. 31, "These criminals had no . . .": Sam Howe Ver-hovek, "'Son of Sam' Law Is Upheld in Jean Harris Case," *New York Times*, May 8, 1991, B4.

p. 33, "In all, victims . . .": Editorial, "Opinion Blames the Legislators' Misguided Outrage," *Las Vegas Review-Journal*, December 13, 1991, 14B.

p. 33, "The decision asserted . . .": *Riggs v. Palmer*, 22 N.E. 188 (1889). Cited in Kathleen Howe, "Is Free Speech Too High a Price to Pay for Crime?," *Loyola of Los Angeles Entertainment Law Review*, 24, January 26, 2005, 344.

CHAPTER THREE

p. 43, "Protected expression . . .": *Simon & Schuster, Inc. v. Fischetti et al.*, 916 F.2d 777, 59 USLW 2234, 18 Media L. Rep. 1187 (US Ct. of Appeals, 2nd Circuit, 1990).

p. 44, "Our society rightly . . .": *Simon & Schuster, Inc. v. Fischetti et al.*

pp. 44–45, "It lessened . . .": *Simon & Schuster, Inc. v. Fischetti et al.*

p. 45, "By upholding . . .": *Simon & Schuster, Inc. v. Fischetti et al.*

p. 46, "At the age . . .": Nicholas Pileggi, *Wiseguy*, New York: Pocket Books/Simon & Schuster, 2010, 17.

p. 46, "Truckloads of swag . . .": Pileggi, *Wiseguy*, 353.

p. 47, "I never saw Paulie . . .": Pileggi, *Wiseguy*, 169.

p. 49, "It is clear . . .": *Simon & Schuster, Inc. v. Fischetti et al.*

p. 49, "The law also . . .": *Simon & Schuster, Inc. v. Fischetti et al.*

p. 49, "Regulations which . . .": *Simon & Schuster, Inc. v. Fischetti et al.*

CHAPTER FOUR

pp. 55–56, "Review is . . .": Ruth Marcus, "High Court to Hear Challenge to 'Son of Sam' Law," *Washington Post*, February 20, 1991, C1.

p. 56, "The AAP argued . . .": Marcus, "High Court to Hear Challenge to 'Son of Sam' Law."

pp. 56–57, "In the wake . . .": Marcus, "High Court to Hear Challenge to 'Son of Sam' Law."

p. 58, "Abrams noted . . .": Marcus, "High Court to Hear Challenge to 'Son of Sam' Law."

p. 59, "If there is . . .": *Texas v. Johnson*, 491 U.S. 397 (1989).

p. 60, "The law violated . . .": *U.S. v. Eichman*, 496 U.S. 310 (1990).

p. 64, "The hard fact . . .": Anthony Kennedy, concurrence, *Texas v. Johnson*, 491 U.S. 397 (1989).

p. 64, "He later . . .": Helen J. Knowles, "The Supreme Court as Civic Educator: Free Speech According to Justice Kennedy," *First Amendment Law Review*, vol. 6, 2008, 2.

p. 65, "Freedom of the press . . .": David Souter, dissent, *Cohen v. Cowles Media Co.*, 501 U.S. 663 (1991).

pp. 66–79, "The law, . . .": Oral arguments, *Simon & Schuster, Inc. v. Members of New York State Crime Victims Board*, 502 U.S. 105 (1991).

CHAPTER FIVE

p. 81, "Justice O'Connor acknowledged . . .": Linda Greenhouse, "High Court Upsets Seizing of Profits on Convicts' Books," *New York Times*, December 11, 1991, A1.

p. 82, "The constitutional right . . .": *Cohen v. California*, 403 U.S. 15 (1971). Cited in *Leathers v. Medlock*, 499 U.S. 439 (1991).

pp. 86–87, "We had the . . .": Nicholas Pileggi, *Wiseguy*, New York: Simon & Schuster, 1986, 150–151. Cited in *Simon & Schuster, Inc. v. Members of New York Crime Victims Board*, 502 U.S. 105 (1991).

p. 88, "Regulations which . . .": *Police Department of Chicago v. Mosely*, 408 U.S. 92 (1972). Cited in Justice Anthony Kennedy's concurrence in *Simon & Schuster, Inc. v. Members of New York Crime Victims Board*.

p. 89, "On the core issues . . .": David G. Savage, "Laws Denying Criminals Profits From Stories Voided," *Los Angeles Times*, December 11, 1991, 16.

p. 90, "Attorney Steven Shapiro . . .": Ruth Marcus, "Law Against Felons Profiting From Books, Movies Is Voided," *Washington Post*, December 11, 1991, A1.

p. 90, "Laws like New York's . . .": Editorial. "'Son of Sam' Laws Rightly Reversed," *New York Times*, December 12, 1991, A30.

p. 90, "The Court, . . .": Editorial, "Opinion Blames the

Legislators' Misguided Outrage," *Las Vegas Review-Journal*, December 13, 1991, 14B.

pp. 90–91, "Richard E. Snyder, . . .": Esther B. Fein, "Decision Praised as a Victory for Free Speech Rights," *New York Times*, December 11, 1991, B8.

p. 91, "We said . . .": "Decision Dismays Victims' Advocates," *Deseret News*, December 11, 1991, www.deseretnews.com/article/198358/decision-dismays-victims-advocates.html

p. 91, "I have no . . .": Tim Appelo, "Making a Killing," *Entertainment Weekly*, January 10, 1992, www.ew.com/ew/articles/0,,309152,00.html

p. 91, "Pileggi pointed out . . .": Carper, "Son of Sam Law Struck Down," *Newsday*, December 11, 1991, 6.

p. 91, "If you look . . .": Appelo, "Making a Killing."

p. 92, "In addition to . . .": Carper, "Son of Sam Law Struck Down."

p. 92, "This is just . . .": Meg Cox, "'Sam' Ruling Likely to Spark Media Scramble," *Wall Street Journal*, December 11, 1991, B1.

p. 92, "There is no . . .": Cox, "'Sam' Ruling Likely to Spark Media Scramble."

p. 93, "The more notorious . . .": Cox, "'Sam' Ruling Likely to Spark Media Scramble."

p. 93, "Barbara Leak, the chair . . .": "Decision Dismays Victims' Advocates," *Deseret News*.

p. 94, "Crime victims are left . . .": Marcus, "Law Against Felons Profiting From Books, Movies Is Voided."

p. 94, "My client . . .": Cox, "'Sam' Ruling Likely to Spark Media Scramble."

p. 95, "We didn't really . . .": Appelo, "Making a Killing."

p. 95, "It was a nice . . .": Appelo, "Making a Killing."

CHAPTER SIX

p. 98, "Maas's attorney called the suits . . .": Frank DiGiacomo, "Sammy the Bull Gravano Isn't Squealing All the Way to the Bank," *New York Observer*, January 25, 1998, www.observer.com/node/40085

p. 99, "Attorney Slade R. Metcalf . . .": Business Editors, "New York State Appellate Division Affirms Dismissal of Crime Victims Board Case Against Peter Maas and HarperCollins Publishers," *Business Wire*, March 7, 2000, 1.

p. 99, "California's Supreme Court . . .": E. Gabriel Perle, Mark A. Fischer, and John Taylor Williams, *Perle & Williams on Publishing Law*, third ed., 2004 supplement, New York: Aspen Publishers, 2004, 1-19–1-20.

p. 101, "The court presented . . .": *Keenan v. Superior Court*, 27 Cal. 4th 413, 40 P.3d 718 (2002).

p. 102, "It is very clear . . .": David L. Hudson Jr., "'Son of Sam' Laws," First Amendment Center, March 2007, www.firstamendmentcenter.org/speech/arts/topic.aspx?topic=son_of_sam

p. 103, "Berkowitz says . . .": Serge F. Kovaleski, "Backers

Give 'Son of Sam' Image Makeover," *New York Times*, July 12, 2010, A18.

p. 106, "Without question . . .": Bureau of National Affairs, "Convicted Racketeer's Book Royalties Are Forfeitable Under Ariz. Statutes," *Media Law Reporter*, 31:2, January 14, 2003, http://ipcenter.bna.com/pic2/ip.nsf/id/BNAP-5HNLZL?OpenDocument

p. 106, "I think what . . .": Hudson, " 'Son of Sam' Laws."

p. 107, "might best be . . .": Hudson, " 'Son of Sam' Laws."

p. 108, "The mother of . . .": Dan Ring, "Sale of Prison-made Items by Alfred Gaynor, Convicted Serial Killer, Raises Legislative Issue," *The Republican*, November 21, 2010, www.masslive.com/news/index.ssf/2010/11/sale_of_prison-made_items_by_a.html

p. 108, "Andy Kahan, . . .": Ring, "Sale of Prison-made Items by Alfred Gaynor, Convicted Serial Killer, Raises Legislative Issue."

p. 108, "To attempt . . .": Suna Chang, "The Prodigal 'Son' Returns: An Assessment of Current 'Son of Sam' Laws and the Reality of the Online Murderabilia Marketplace," *Rutgers Computer & Technology Law Journal*, January 1, 2005.

p. 109, "California law . . .": Cal. Civ. Code § 2225, http://codes.lp.findlaw.com/cacode/CIV/5/d3/4/8/s2225

p. 109, "Texas amended . . .": Chang, "The Prodigal 'Son' Returns: An Assessment of Current 'Son of Sam' Laws and the Reality of the Online Murderabilia Marketplace."

p. 110, "Nervous but no . . .": Nick Allen, "Goodfella Henry Hill still living in hiding 20 years after film release," *The Telegraph*, July 23, 2010.

p. 110, "There are some . . .": Pete Samson, "OldFella," *The Sun* [London], August 5, 2010, 22.

p. 111, "I stopped looking . . .": Nick Carroll, "Saga of Henry Hill: a gangster's old habits die hard, *The Berlin Citizen*, January 12, 2011, http://berlin. ctcitizens.com/story/saga-henry-hill-gangsters-old-habits-die-hard

p. 111, "There's always . . .": Allen, "Goodfella Henry Hill still living in hiding 20 years after film release."

p. 111, "I don't give . . .": Heather Alexander, "Mafia King on the Straight and Narrow," E24 show, *BBC News*, March 29, 2008, http://news.bbc.co.uk/2/hi/7319520.stm

pp. 113–114, "Helen Strickland, whose . . .": Laurel J. Sweet, "Victim's Kin Outraged by Killer's Art: Battle to Prevent Prisoner from Cashing in on Crime," *Boston Herald*, November 18, 2005, www.masslive.com/news/index.ssf/2010/11/sale_of_prison-made_items_by_a.html

p. 114 "For some, you . . .": Bill Zajac, "Prisoners' Art Poses

Tough Legal Questions," *The Republican*, December 12, 2005, www.15yearstolife.com/Artban.htm

p. 114, "The discovery . . .": Anthony Papa, "Support the Arts in Prison," 15 Years to Life, www.15yearstolife.com/Artban.htm. Cited in Chang, "The Prodigal 'Son' Returns: An Assessment of Current 'Son of Sam' Laws and the Reality of the Online Murderabilia Marketplace."

p. 114, "Creating and selling . . .": Anthony Papa, "Support the Arts in Prison," 15 Years to Life, www.15yearstolife.com/Artban.htm

p. 115, "First, he says, . . .": Ronald S. Rauchberg, e-mail message to author, April 7, 2011.

p. 116, "However much . . .": Martin Garbus, "Let's Do Away with 'Son of Sam' Laws," *Publishers Weekly*, February 13, 1995, www.accessmylibrary.com/article-1G1-16516069/let-do-away-son.html

FURTHER INFORMATION

AUDIO/VIDEO

Irons, Peter, ed. *May It Please the Court: Courts, Kids, and the Constitution*. New York: New York Press, 2000 (audio).

BOOKS

Conway, John Richard. *A Look at the First Amendment: Freedom of Speech and Religion*. Berkeley Heights, NJ: Myreportlinks.com, 2008.

Engdahl, Sylvia, *Free Speech*. San Diego: Greenhaven Press, 2007.

Fridell, Ron. *U.S. v. Eichman: Flag Burning and Free Speech*. New York: Marshall Cavendish, 2008.

Gold, Susan Dudley. *Parody of Public Figures: Hustler Magazine Inc. v. Falwell*. New York: Cavendish Square, 2014.

———. *Tinker v. Des Moines: Free Speech for Students*. New York: Marshall Cavendish Benchmark, 2006.

Jones, Molly. *The First Amendment: Freedom of Speech, the Press, and Religion*. New York: Rosen Central, 2011.

MacDonald, Joan Vos. *Religion and Free Speech Today: A Pro/Con Debate*. Berkeley Heights, NJ: Enslow Publishers, 2008.

Steffens, Bradley. *Free Speech*. Yankton, SD: Erickson Press, 2007.

WEBSITES

American Civil Liberties Union
www.aclu.org

FindLaw (U.S. Supreme Court Cases)
www.findlaw.com/casecode/supreme.html

First Amendment Center
www.firstamendmentcenter.org

Law Library, American Law and Legal Information
http://law.jrank.org

Legal Information Institute, Cornell University
Law School
www.law.cornell.edu

Oyez Project, U.S. Supreme Court Multimedia website
www.oyez.org

Reporters Committee for Freedom of the Press
www.rcfp.org

Supreme Court Historical Society
www.supremecourthistory.org

Supreme Court of the United States
www.supremecourt.gov

BIBLIOGRAPHY

ARTICLES

Alexander, Heather. "Mafia King on the Straight and Narrow," E24 show, *BBC News*, March 29, 2008, http://news.bbc.co.uk/2/hi/7319520.stm

Allen, Nick. "Goodfella Henry Hill Still Living in Hiding 20 Years after Film Release," *The Telegraph*, July 23, 2010, www.telegraph.co.uk/news

Appelo, Tim. "Making a Killing," *Entertainment Weekly*, January 10, 1992, www.ew.com/ew/article/0,,309152,00.html

Bureau of National Affairs, "Convicted Racketeer's Book Royalties Are Forfeitable Under Ariz. Statutes," *Media Law Reporter*, 31:2, January 14, 2003.

Business Editors. "New York State Appellate Division Affirms Dismissal of Crime Victims Board Case Against Peter Maas and HarperCollins Publishers," *Business Wire*, March 7, 2000, 1.

Canby, Vincent. "A Cold-Eyed Look at the Mob's Inner Workings," *New York Times*, September 19, 1990, www.nytimes.com/1990/09/19/movies/review-film-a-cold-eyed-look-at-the-mob-s-inner-workings.html

Carper, Alison. "Son of Sam Law Struck Down," *Newsday*, December 11, 1991, 6.

Carroll, Nick. "Saga of Henry Hill: A Gangster's Old Habits Die Hard," *The Berlin Citizen*, January 12, 2011, http://berlin.ctcitizens.com

Chang, Suna. "The Prodigal 'Son' Returns: An Assessment of Current 'Son of Sam' Laws and the Reality of the Online Murderabilia Marketplace," *Rutgers Computer & Technology Law Journal*, January 1, 2005.

Cox, Meg. "'Sam' Ruling Likely to Spark Media Scramble," *Wall Street Journal*, December 11, 1991, B1.

"Criminals' Revenues from Stories Curbed," *New York Times*, August 13, 1977, http://query.nytimes.com/mem/archive/pdf?res=F50D1FFA345F167493C1A81783D85F438785F9

"Decision Dismays Victims' Advocates," *Deseret News*, December 11, 1991, www.deseretnews.com

DiGiacomo, Frank. "Sammy the Bull Gravano Isn't Squealing All the Way to the Bank," *New York Observer*, January 25, 1998, www.observer.com

Ebert, Roger. "GoodFellas," *Chicago Sun Times*, September 2, 1990, http://rogerebert.suntimes.com

Editorial, "Opinion Blames the Legislators' Misguided Outrage," *Las Vegas Review-Journal*, December 13, 1991, 14B.

Editorial, "'Son of Sam' Laws Rightly Reversed," *New York Times*, December 12, 1991, A30.

Editorial, "U.S. Supreme Court Rejects 'Son of Sam' Law on Profits," *San Antonio Express-News*, December 11, 1991, 15A.

Fein, Esther B. "Decision Praised as a Victory for Free

Speech Rights," *New York Times*, December 11, 1991, B8.

Garbus, Martin. "Let's Do Away with 'Son of Sam' Laws," *Publishers Weekly*, February 13, 1995.

Greenhouse, Linda. "High Court Upsets Seizing of Profits on Convicts' Books," *New York Times*, December 11, 1991, A1.

Hernandez, Raymond. "7 Prisoners Get Clemency From Pataki," *New York Times*, December 24, 1996, B4.

Howe, Kathleen. "Is Free Speech Too High a Price to Pay for Crime?" *Loyola of Los Angeles Entertainment Law Review*, 24, January 26, 2005, 344.

Hudson, David L. Jr., "'Son of Sam' Laws," First Amendment Center, March 2007, www.first amendmentcenter.com

Knowles, Helen J. "The Supreme Court as Civic Educator: Free Speech According to Justice Kennedy," First Amendment Law Review, 6, 2008.

Kovaleski, Serge F. "Backers Give 'Son of Sam' Image Makeover," *New York Times*, July 12, 2010, A18.

Lehmann-Haupt, Christopher. "Books of the Times: Wiseguy: Life in a Mafia Family," *New York Times*, January 16, 1986, www.nytimes.com/1986/01/16/ books/books-of-the-times634886.html?scp=2&sq= Nicholas+Pileggi&st=nyt

Linfield, Susan. "'GoodFellas' Looks at the Banality of Mob Life," *New York Times*, September 16, 1990, www.nytimes.com/1990/09/16/movies/film-good-fellas-looks-at-the-banality-of-mob-life.html

McElroy, Wendy. "Henry Thoreau and 'Civil Disobedience,'"Thoreau Reader, Future of Freedom Foundation, 2005. http://thoreau.eserver.org/wendy.html

Marcus, Ruth. "High Court to Hear Challenge to 'Son of Sam' Law," *Washington Post*, February 20, 1991, C1.

———. "Law Against Felons Profiting From Books, Movies Is Voided," *Washington Post*, December 11, 1991, A1.

"Offensive material policy," eBay, http://pages.ebay.com/help/policies/offensive.html

Papa, Anthony. "Support the Arts in Prison," 15 Years to Life, www.15yearstolife.com/Artban.htm

Patrick, Vincent. "Not-so-organized Crime," *New York Times*, January 26, 1986, www.nytimes.com/1986/01/26/books/not-so-organized-crime.html

Ring, Dan. "Sale of Prison-made Items by Alfred Gaynor, Convicted Serial Killer, Raises Legislative Issue," *The Republican*, November 21, 2010, www.masslive.com

Samson, Pete. "OldFella," *The Sun* [London], August 5, 2010, 22.

Savage, David G. "Laws Denying Criminals Profits From Stories Voided," *Los Angeles Times*, December 11, 1991, 16.

Smith, Greg B. "Kin of Gravano's Victims Get 420g in Payback," *New York Daily News*, July 22, 2004, http://articles.nydailynews.com/2004-07-22/news/18283132_1_gravano-sammy-bull-attorney-ron-kuby

Stone, Geoffrey R. "Rehnquist's Legacy Doesn't Measure Up," *Chicago Tribune*, September 6, 2005, www.law.uchicago.edu/news/stone090605

Streitfeld, David. "The Cash Course in Crime Writing," *Washington Post*, December 11, 1991, C1.

Sweet, Laurel J. "Victim's Kin Outraged by Killer's Art: Battle to Prevent Prisoner from Cashing in on Crime," *Boston Herald*, November 18, 2005, www.masslive.com

Verhovek, Sam Howe. "'Son of Sam' Law Is Upheld in Jean Harris Case," *New York Times*, May 8, 1991, B4.

Zajac, Bill. "Prisoners' Art Poses Tough Legal Questions," *The Republican*, December 12, 2005, www.15yearstolife.com/Artban.htm

BOOKS

Perle, E. Gabriel, Mark A. Fischer, and John Taylor Williams. *Perle & Williams on Publishing Law*, 3rd ed., 2004 supplement. New York: Aspen Publishers, 2004.

Pileggi, Nicholas. *Wiseguy*. New York: Simon & Schuster/Pocket Books, 1986, 2010.

COURT CASES

Arizona v. Gravano, 60 P.3d 246, 248-49 (2002).

Arkansas Writers' Project, Inc. v. Ragland, 481 U.S. 221 (1987).

Boos v. Barry, 485 U.S. 312 (1988).

Bouchard v. Price, 694 A.2d 670 (R.I. 1997).

Caplin & Drysdale, Chartered v. United States, 491 U.S. 617 (1989).

Cohen v. California, 403 U.S. 15 (1971).

Cohen v. Cowles Media Company, 501 U.S. 663 (1991).

Commonwealth v. Power, 420 Mass. 410 (1995); 116 S.Ct. 698 (1996).

Keenan v. Superior Court, 27 Cal. 4th 413, 40 P.3d 718 (2002). www.aele.org/law/2002JBMAY/kvs.html

Leathers v. Medlock, 499 U.S. 439 (1991).

Meyer v. Grant, 486 U.S. 414 (1988).

Near v. Minnesota, 283 U.S. 697 (1931).

New York State Victims Board v. J.J.M. Productions, Inc., N.Y. App. Div. No. 1380, March 7, 2000.

Opinion of the Justices to the Senate, SJC-08634, 436 Mass. 1201; 764 N.E.2d 343; 2002 Mass. (March 14, 2002).

Petrie v. Chase Manhattan Bank, 38 AD 2d 206, NY (1972).

Police Department of Chicago v. Mosely, 408 U.S. 92 (1972).

Regan v. Time, 468 U.S. 641 (1984).

Republican Party of Minnesota v. White, 536 U.S. 765 (2002).

Riggs v. Palmer, 22 N.E. 188 (1889).

Schenck v. United States, 249 U.S. 47 (1919).

Shapiro v. Thompson, 394 U.S. 618 (1969).

Simon & Schuster, Inc. v. Fischetti et al., 916 F.2d 777, 59 USLW 2234, 18 Media L. Rep. 1187 (US Ct. of Appeals, 2nd Circuit, 1990).

Simon & Schuster, Inc. v. Members of New York State Crime Victims Board, 502 U.S. 105 (1991).

Texas v. Johnson, 491 U.S. 397 (1989).

United States v. Eichman, 496 U.S. 310 (1990).

United States v. O'Brien (1968).

West Virginia v. Barnette, 319 U.S. 624 (1943).

INTERVIEW

Rauchberg, Ronald S. Interview with author, April 7, 2011.

STATUTES

Cal. Civ. Code § 2225, http://codes.lp.findlaw.com/cacode/CIV/5/d3/4/8/s2225

N.Y. Exc. Law § 632-a: NY Code—Section 632-A: Crime victims, http://codes.lp.findlaw.com/nycode/EXC/22/632-a

INDEX

Page numbers in **boldface** are photographs.

ABOUT THE AUTHOR

Susan Dudley Gold has worked as a reporter for a daily newspaper, managing editor of two statewide business magazines, and freelance editor and writer for several regional publications. She has written more than four dozen books for middle-school and high-school students on a variety of topics.

Her work, which includes series on American history and law, has won numerous awards, including Carter G. Woodson Honor Book, Notable Social Studies Trade Book for Young People, and several first-place awards in the National Federation of Press Women's communications contest. Her most recent books include several titles in the Landmark Legislation series, including *Americans with Disabilities Act* and *Freedom of Information Act*, and the four other books in this series. Gold is the author of a number of books on Maine history.

She and her husband, John Gold, own and operate a web design and publishing business in Maine. They have one son, Samuel; a granddaughter, Callie; and a grandson, Alexander.